ROMAN COINS AND
HOW TO COLLECT THEM

JOHN F. FOX

ROMAN COINS AND HOW TO COLLECT THEM

LONGMAN
LONDON AND NEW YORK

Longman Group Limited
Longman House, Burnt Mill, Harlow
Essex CM20 2JE, England
Associated companies throughout the world

Published in the United States of America
by Longman Inc., New York

First published 1983

British Library Cataloguing in Publication Data

Fox, John F.
  Roman coins and how to collect them.
  1. Coins, Roman
  I. Title
  737.4937   CJ833

  ISBN 0-582-50309-4

Library of Congress Cataloging in Publication Data

Fox, John F., 1942–
  Roman coins and how to collect them.

  Includes index.
  1. Coins, Roman – Collectors and collecting.
  I. Title.
  CJ837.F69   1983   737.4937′075   82-20363
  ISBN 0-582-50309-4 (pbk.)

Set in 10/11 pt Baskerville, Linotron 202
Printed in Hong Kong by
Astros Printing Ltd.

CONTENTS

PART III COLLECTORS' WORKING INFORMATION

NOTE ON DENOMINATION NAMES AND MEASUREMENTS

Discussion continues about the names of many Roman denominations. Traditional names are employed in the body of this book. For a closer scrutiny of the background to these terms, the reader is referred to the section on denominations in Ch. II and to The Roman denominations on p. 168.

The Greek spelling has been retained for the *drachma* and its various multiples; likewise, in so far as it is possible to transliterate Hebrew, the Hebrew spelling of *shekel* and *prutah* has been retained; for silver and copper in use in Palestine under Roman occupation, the traditional Greek terms *tetradrachmon* (or *stater*) and *lepton* have been used.

Many coins in the book have been considerably enlarged from actual size. The following approximate range of measurements may assist the reader in examining the illustrations.

sestertius and *double-sestertius*	− 30−35 mm (later, as low as 25 mm)
as dupondius and *large follis*	− 25−30 mm
semis	− 20−22 mm
quadrans	− 15−18 mm
denarius, argenteus and *siliqua*	− 18−20 mm
antoninianus	− 22 mm descending (later, as low as 5 mm in some areas)
ae 2, 3, 4.	− 22 mm, 18 mm, 15 mm.
tetradrachmon (*shekel*)	− 22−25 mm
lepton (*prutah*)	− 15−18 mm
hemidrachma (silver)	− 15 mm

Prices shown reflect the range a collector is likely to meet.

AUTHOR'S ACKNOWLEDGEMENTS

The flaws in this book are mine; many of its better points are owed to others. Ron Smith of the Oxford Coin Centre has patiently supplied me with coins, information and financial sympathy over the years and entrusted me with his portion of the Bath Hoard. Raymond Sancroft-Baker and Richard Bishop gave me a warm welcome at Christie's and Richard Bishop in particular gave his time most generously in reading the manuscript. Without his constructive criticism and the further labours put in by Peter and Nigel Finch of Oxford, drawing on their years of collecting experience, this book would not have been possible.

Paul and Italo Vecchi of Vecchi and Sons, London, could not have been more unstinting in their help with photographs and affording me the hospitality of their premises; the notes and illustrations in their auction catalogues (formerly with Bonhams, now with Schwer) are arguably the finest produced in England.

Thanks are also due to Su-Z Kono of Superior Coin and Stamp Company, Beverley Hills, California; David Millar, their former European representative (now trading independently); Stanley Gibbons Magazines Ltd and Christie's for the use of certain other photographs. The Ashmolean Museum, The British Museum, the National Museum of Wales, and the BBC Hulton Picture Library kindly supplied further illustrations and gave permission for their use. My colleagues Peter Hampson, Charles Stanikowski and William Lind take credit for the hitherto unpublished material while Carterton Laboratories and particularly Benjamin Ruscombe-King of Oxford produced the end results. I have seen the camera defy the old proverb and actually turn sows' ears into silk purses.

No writer on Roman coins can take off without the solid runways of scholarship laid down in the past. I owe a great debt to Milne and Kraay's *Catalogue of Coins of Alexandria in the Ashmolean Museum*, to Meshorer's *Jewish Coins of the Second Temple Period*, to Grant's *Roman Imperial Coinage*, Sutherland's *Coinage and Currency in Roman Britain*, the *British Archeological Report, No. 4, 1974* and Shiel's *Episode of Carausius and Allectus*. The books described in Chapter IV are also in many cases owed a debt, not least the volumes of the *Roman Imperial Coins* (*RIC*) brought right up to the present day with the addition of Dr Kent's

Volume VIII on the *Family of Constantine* (1981). Besides the books which have worn grooves in my collector's bookshelf, there are many articles and books of which the content has become part of my mental furniture over the years while the title and author has long since been forgotten. To these too I acknowledge my debt.

Many people have shown individual kindnesses, too numerous to be listed exhaustively: David Hood of Oxfam for his many warm welcomes and courtesies; Ingrid Gassmann and Nadine Strange for remembering 'him and his coins' when abroad in Israel; my pupils for 'suffering' my coins from time to time; Roger Box of Andoversford for pages of notes and memories as well as some interesting material at a budget collector's price; Paul Cartwright of Bicester for supplying the cleaning formula described on p. 180; Frank Scollen for making material available from his 'archive' of historical memorabilia.

Above all, I thank my family – Glen, Karl, Mark and Daniel – whose loving and humourous support has fuelled my numismomania.

ACKNOWLEDGEMENTS

The author is grateful to the following for permission to use and for supplying copyright photographs:

Vecchi and Sons, London for Figs 10b, 14, 16, 17a & b, 18, 23b, 24, 25b, 27, 28, 29, 31b, 33a–e, 34a, 35, 37, 44b, 45, 49g & h, 58b, 59a, 61b, 62a–c, 67a,b,d, & e, 69, 70b–d, 71b & d, 72a(ii) & b(ii); 73d & e, 75, 76, 77b & c, 78, 80b, 81b, 83b, 85b, 87b, 89b, 90, 92c, 101c, 107c, 108b & c, 109b, 111, 114b, 116, 118b & c, 119a, 122, 123, 126, 127b, 130, 133, 135, 136c, 137, 139, 140, 143a & c, 144, 145, 146b, and 149; Christie's, London for Figs 13 and 86b; Ashmolean Museum, Oxford for Figs 3, 15, 19a, 20b, 21a & b, 72a, 109c, 110a, b & d, 136a and 148; National Museum of Wales, Cardiff for Fig. 38; Superior Stamp and Coin Co., Inc., California for Fig. 105; Stanley Gibbons Magazines Limited for Fig. 104; BBC Hulton Picture Library for Fig. 117.

Fig. 126 is reproduced by courtesy of the Trustees of the British Museum.

All other illustrations belong to the author and are his copyright.

Acknowledgement is due to Penguin Books Ltd for the translation of excerpts from Juvenal, *The Sixteen Satires*; Josephus, *The Jewish War*; Eusebius, *Church History*; Anon, *Lives of The Later Caesars*.

Excerpts from Suetonius, Pliny Senior and the Greek and Latin of the New Testament are in the author's own translation.

Silver, by reason of its cleanness, unaptness to rust, ponderousness etc was pitched upon to be an universal pledge of all commerce about 488 years after the Flood.

And to have the trouble of weighing and assaying every piece received which would greatly obstruct the dispatch of business, it became customary for princes to give such and such stamps to the several denominations or quantities of silver. The antiquity of which stamping money (which we call coin) we can trace no further back than the Romans' time, among whom, the ingenious Mr Vaughan of Grays Inn tells us, Servius Tullius was the first.

Edward Hatton, *The Tradesman's Treasury* (1695). Annotated copy of Edward Howarth and John Taylor, Rochdale merchants, now in the author's possession.

INTRODUCTION

Numismatics has come a long way since Edward Hatton and Mr Vaughan of Gray's Inn! Perhaps they were 'gannets', curious and knowledgeable collectors of all manner of coin. The collecting 'bug' at least has not changed, even if our knowledge of the subject has.

This book is written to help a growing band of enthusiasts smitten with an interest in things Roman, in particular coins. The symptoms of the 'affliction' are too well known to collectors (and families) to need describing here.

Why should the number of Roman coin collectors be *increasing*? At first sight it might seem to be a small, rarified and inevitably shrinking corner of the market. Surely, supplies dried up in the fifth century?

Strangely enough, the opposite is true. The market is constantly being nourished, as this book shows. For instance, the metal detector, whatever may be thought of that transistorised ferret, has brought thousands of coins to the surface in recent years and created new collectors in the act.

In the early 1980s German dealers noticed a glut of Byzantine coins coming on to the market. Was this evidence of an unknown Byzantine subculture in medieval Europe? Or was it the work of some skilled forger deep in a Salzkammergut hideaway? The facts were more prosaic. Turkish *gastarbeiter* in Germany had seen the demand for antiquities in Europe. From their earnings they despatched metal detectors back to their home villages. Word was passed round and in some places, at least, coin and artefact harvests began to take the place of the (equally illegal) white poppy or the legal but less immediately rewarding olive crop.

A wave of nostalgia has surged over our age of glass and concrete. The old has a new popularity. It may be to do with the approach of AD 2000. It may be a yearning for the apparent stability before the wars, high-speed technology and inflation. We certainly look twice at anything old. Attics are being emptied more carefully. Auctioneers handle far more Roman material from deceased effects than they do from the finds of the metal detector. Long-hidden collections and accumulations are seeing daylight again, old jackdaw nests with their inevitable mixture of treasure and dross.

The expansion of education, increased travel and telecommunications have made us all aware of the value placed on history in every sense. (Not long ago, a general dealer tried to sell me a handful of worn Roman bronzes with some enthusiasm for a 'killing'. 'The big ones is BC and the little ones is AD – and they're bloody old, I can tell you!')

There is more leisure time, some of it due to unemployment or early retirement, some of it brought about by changes in working hours. There may not be much more money to spend along with the time, but there are hobbies – Roman coin collecting is one – where *some* of the material has actually cheapened over the years, offering greater opportunities to those with limited means. Popular scholarship has also done much to enable a collector to deepen his knowledge even without the privilege of formal education in the Classics.

Once a collector starts in any field, he tends to move away from the overcrowded general areas to find a corner which he can master within a foreseeable time. Collectors' shops and postal sales have mushroomed to meet and foster the many varieties of this demand. The railway arches at London's Charing Cross, to give one example, are almost totally given over to shops for every different type of coin. The new interest has even spread to charities which now appeal for coins, exchanging them for (current) cash from collectors' pockets to meet the needs of a good cause.

The response to such appeals is astounding, coming to the warehouses as it does each day by the containerload. From biscuit tins, old sewing boxes, envelopes and Victorian leather purses rotting at the seams come campaign medals, broken jewellery, Maundy Money, loot from both wars and, of course, the coins. Forgers' florins and electrotype 'ancients' nestle among Tudor and Spanish silver; half-sovereigns lie camouflaged among mint-lustre farthings. Like the rats of Hamelin there is every conceivable coin, some inconceivable ones – and they pour into the depots in thousands.

Volunteers give time in exchange for dust on the breath and filth on the fingers. They sift through boxes spilling over with currency notes, the bulk of it the limp, dead money of forgotten and sometimes tragic regimes. They scoop pre-decimal coppers from tea-chests into 15 kg bags and common foreign coins into 12 kg bags; current material goes to the banks for redemption.

Among all this modern financial flotsam a handful of ancients invariably appears during a typical hour of sorting – a Punic copper, a plated *denarius*, a Gordian III *antoninianus*, an Egyptian *tetradrachmon* of Diocletian, a worn *dupondius* of Vespasian, oddments 'from the Beachy Head Hoard', a provincial bronze of Philip I and several modern copies with their edge-seams left unfiled.

As the warehouse scene may suggest, the world of coins is vast and one collector's experience is always limited. Republican Rome and Byzantium receive only passing mention in this book. My primary interest and that, I suspect, of most Roman collectors is the Imperial period, a stage alive with personalities and packed with events. I have chosen three Roman provinces for special consideration – Egypt, Palestine and Britain have long held my interest. Collectors may enjoy my high-speed excursions across the history of these territories.

Most of the coins in this book are reproduced larger than life to simulate for the reader the view through the magnifying glass. The centuries have taken their toll of every coin illustrated and I have deliberately included damaged and worn coins of interest – the only condition in which many collectors might hope to own them. There are few expensive coins in my own collection of 'damaged rarities' but then collecting is about an interest in history rather than an investment.

A disembodied hand appears from offstage in some photographs. It provides scale and an indicator. The understanding reader will know that it is also a trademark of the profession to which the writer belongs. I often use the coins in this book for teaching. Those in the world of education may find its chapters and Suggestions for teachers on p. 181 of particular interest. More generally, it is hoped that the book will prompt collectors of every level, but particularly the 'budget collector', to turn back to their own coins with a fresh pair of eyes while at the same time suggesting to new collectors that Roman coins provide a field full of interest, not too far removed from our own world.

PART I

THE ROMAN COIN

I

THE ROMAN COIN COLLECTOR

> One millionaire was so nervous about his Phrygian marbles, his priceless treasures, his amber and ivory knick-nacks, his tortoiseshell objêts d'art that he kept a vast squad of servants with water bucket on duty all night. But the tub of the naked cynic Diogenes never caught fire; if it broke he could pick up another.
>
> **Juvenal, *Satire XIV*, c. AD 130**

How it all starts

My answer to 'Why Roman coins?' is, I suspect, interesting if disjointed. It begins, as does the story of many of our interests, in the first encounters of childhood. Coins galore of every shape and date filled tins and boxes along with the usual toys. A family friend then presented me with a large brown coin and said it was Roman (Fig. 1). Aged about seven, I did not know what that meant but I saw that the coin was not quite round like the others. I distinctly remember a fellow-feeling with whoever made it because it was so close to my own attempts at that stage in life to draw anything circular.

On one side it had a stern soldierly face (with just the ghost of a smile?), like the picture of the sentry at Pompeii which by then had caught my childhood imagination. A Victorian painter had portrayed

1. *Follis*, Maximian, first reign AD 286–305, Section **3 SIS(cia)** mint. Genius of the Roman People.

him at the city gate, 'Faithful unto Death', the ash piling up against his sandals and the glare of the eruption lighting up a controlled fear on his face. The coin was idealised propaganda; the picture was sentimentalised morality. At the time I knew neither of those things; I did know that both were linked to the word *Rome*.

In damp and windy Lancashire all that Rome meant to us as children was a cobbled marching track over the moors at Blackstone Edge, the couch grass sprouting between its sets and wheel-grooves. Perhaps too, it meant day excursions to York or Chester and silent piles of cream or red stone, the remains of Roman garrison centres. Much further to the north, where the clouds scudded from over the Pennine horizon, we had read that there was a great wall, a seventy mile long sentry walk, overgrown but intact, a witness to something great in our past. Invariably we muddled it with the Great Wall of China.

My own family had been with the Army since 1877, serving in outposts as far apart as Newfoundland and India. I felt a small boy's empathy with those kilted legionaries whom I pictured roughing it on our windswept English highlands, manning this outpost of their own Empire. Then, when the time came to go to boarding-school, the legionaries' not-quite-round bronze stayed in a tin with the other coins and with childhood.

School was a Spartan experience, a postwar Dotheboys Hall, run on a heady cocktail of hard work, religiosity and bad food. 'Gentlemen' were not really expected to study the sciences. The result was that a whole world of the bygone classics was opened to us – Latin and Greek against a backdrop of Ancient History. We left school knowing much about Athens and Rome. I even had my coin identified as a *follis* of Maximian from about AD 300. It had also 'bred' a superb small bronze of Constantius, found in a study inkwell – my first experience of archaeology (Fig. 2). Like its predecessor, *follis*-junior was not quite round either.

2. *Ae 3*, possibly known as **centenionalis**, Constantius II as Caesar AD 324–37, Section **1 AL(exandria)** mint. Soldiers guard standards; Constantius is also in armour.

After Sparta came Rome, literally. I spent a number of years in that city, the home of my two bronze coins. Romano-British traffic has always been two-way although the books make far more of the Romans coming one way to Britain. Caradog (Caratacus) died out there as an emperor's hostage. Alfred, Edward the Confessor, Macbeth and Harold of England spent time in the city, either as scholars or as pilgrims. The Stuarts in exile found their last resting place beneath St Peter's, hard by the tomb of the Breakspear Pope (Adrian IV) from St Albans. The defiant Ulster earls ended their flight from Ireland in tombs on the Janiculum Hill. Less importantly and more anonymously I studied there in one of the old recusant colleges dating back to penal days.

Rome is a city of broken pillars and frantic everyday living. It is cushioned against earthquakes by a cantilever of buried ruins and tunnels. Its fleamarkets abound with coins brought in daily by the navvy, the linesman and the farm-worker. In the 1960s coins also featured in the now popular accounts of the search under St Peter's itself for the grave of the Galilean fisherman. (They found his grave but mislaid the bones in a dramatic comedy worthy of Don Camillo set to a score by Verdi.) Coins, too, loomed large in the new studies of Biblical archaeology and early church history as the science of numismatics joined practically every other science in re-interpreting old beliefs for the modern world.

Everywhere you go in Rome there appear those same coin-type busts – in gardens, ruins, courtyards and embedded in walls – muscular necks and staring eyes, chipped chins and broken noses, firm jawlines and severe (if curly) military hairstyles. In a backyard on the Capitol lurks a giant statue of Constantine, or at least his head, leg and hand. Behind and above him stands an earlier broken inscription about *Britannia* – all that remains of the monument to the invasion of Britain in AD 43. (Fig. 3).

3. *Denarius*, Claudius, AD 46. Two arches were erected for the British victory, one at Rome and one apparently at Boulogne. **De Britann** abbreviated a long inscription (now fragments) recording defeat of 'eleven British kings . . . across the Ocean'.

While the ghosts of Pius IX and Garibaldi still cast gloom over Rome, the more recently dead Mussolini also played poltergeist with everyday life. To enhance the Fascist capital of the proposed new Italian Empire, he had tried to resurrect the old Rome. Ruins were unearthed and reconstructed. They got in the way of living and working. They bred rats, housed wild cats and obstructed traffic. They also had the total protection of law, long after the Fascist lawmakers were dead. A new underground railway had to be re-routed every time it came up against buried ruins. Its rails now run through tunnels of glass cases. At least the workmen had a reasonable hope of finding gold. Anything else (like mosaics) they reburied. 'History has taken care of itself,' one explained, 'we have to look after ourselves.' One exception was the Roman coin. It used to be worth defying the rigid discipline of the time, taking a forbidden trip out to buy some of their finds from the rummage trays of the market.

Below where I lived was a network of cellars. Some even contained human bones, still unburied from tombs desecrated during the French invasion of 1798. Old surveys of the surrounding area seemed to suggest the site had held a barracks of chariot-racers from the Circus. Even Tacitus offered a clue that they had been built by the spendthrift Emperor Vitellius in AD 69. The earthpacked floors, untouched since the Middle Ages, were crying out to be 'read'. After words in the right quarters we decided to dig. Enthusiasm grew as the first coin surfaced amid first-century foundations (Fig. 4).

4. *Sestertius*, Domitian, AD 86. Copper droplets on the surface came from nearby items melted by fire; the reverse, like that in Fig. 21b), is similarly largely obliterated.

We worked for about two months in tin hats and half light, breathing in bad air and dust. The remains which emerged could not exactly be proved to be a jockeys' barracks or anything else for that matter, save large and first century AD. I can still feel now the thrill of handling that *sestertius*, the first and finest of a number of coins to surface. This time it was much more rounded, almost like a presentation piece. It was a touchpiece bridging the gap of fifty or more dead generations. (Shortly afterwards, a distinguished writer who shall remain nameless breathed over it the unforgettable words 'absolutely *delicious!*'). However the experience is described, it poses the questions behind every ancient coin. Who held it last? Who lost it, failed to retrieve it and walked away all those years ago?

There were other adventures in archaeology to blunt the sharper edges of life but none of them produced coins. I remember helping a professor drag a sunken Roman pillar from a lakebed on a hot summer afternoon; his garden where we sat recovering that evening was the former graveyard of the Legion II *Parthica* once based nearby. One winter, someone telephoned to ask me to come and identify a tunnel of running water which had suddenly yawned open beneath their cellar floor. A long crawl with freezing water running through trousers and shirt established that it was an aqueduct from Imperial times still taking fresh water into the city two millennia later. In the same cellar was the cobwebbed and bricked up entrance to a quarter-mile tunnel heading out towards the Colosseum; in 1944, on the Pope's orders, Jews were hidden there from the SS in the streets above – a curious irony since the Colosseum itself was Europe's first slave-labour camp for Jews after AD 70.

One day, making the most of hot summer months spent in enforced lethargy, we explored a cave in the hills near Rome. The cave floor yielded an arsenal of live wartime flak ammunition. After exercising great care (and timidity) with heaps of 30 mm shells, we came upon a rusty cylinder which an 'expert' identified as 'probably an anti-personnel device'. We were fools enough to think of detonating it: we looked even more foolish when we eventually found we were handling a tin of Wehrmacht-issue cheese spread dated 1944. Perhaps more aesthetically exciting, workmen some years later lowered me down on a cable into a shaft just prior to capping a well. A cold and muddy shape in the silt turned out to be a broken marble Eros astride a bucking dolphin (Fig. 5).

5. From a Roman well. Eros riding a dolphin, mistaken at first sight by the pump-operator for 'a boy riding a horse backwards'! (10 cm).

And so, almost unintentionally, I began to collect Roman coins. I now use them occasionally for teaching in a comprehensive school. They fascinate fourteen-year olds and provoke eighteen-year olds to think. They tell an old story in a new way to adults. Sure enough, the

comment is sometimes made, 'Not very circular, are they?' Rummage
bowls in the Jerusalem market, Arab boys digging in Samaria, friends
bringing presents from abroad, oddments from junkboxes, collectors
and dealers have given me a lively and relatively inexpensive hobby,
not to mention a professional teaching-aid. The coins are back almost
in regular use. They also provide therapy, enjoyment and what I call
'armchair archaeology'. I sometimes mount them in small frames as
presents. Gardening at home or digging in with a Territorial unit on
Salisbury Plain, the smell of the earth brings back by association the
thrill of those first Roman coins – although the only finds now are old
buttons, washers or at best a galleon half-penny.

The earth holds our archives. It may lack an index but it does move
its contents around – they do not just lie there. The earthworm turns
over several tons in his life. The farmer ploughs every year. Our town
services nearly all run underground. Plants, trees and rain turn the soil
continuously. Children and footballers churn up the ground – a col-
league once picked up a Marcus Aurelius copper from a rugby touch-
line (Fig. 6). It should not surprise us that some of these secrets appear
from time to time as the earth operates its own 'Thirty Year Ruling'.
Roman coins form one of the larger parts of that deposit. Ancient Rome
may seem far away in both years and miles (even the latter are named
after the thousand paces of the Roman soldier), but it still holds our
roots just as a man's line of growth can be traced back to some cot or
playpen.

6. *As*, Marcus Aurelius, AD 164. Mars strides across the reverse with spear and
trophy; Marcus is in armour with the title **Armeniacus**.

Collector or investor?

I am an amateur numismatist with no commercial connections. I write
for readers perhaps in a similar position, on an average income with
a family to be fed. Can a collection be regarded as an investment as
well, like some of our more publicised national pension funds which
have invested heavily in the arts? Or is that simply a subtle way of
trying to justify a plain addiction from which we do not admit we suffer? Certainly good quality Roman coins will never lose their value,
whatever the rate of inflation. They can be resold at any time with
profit to spare.

The problem with the pure investor is that he must be ready and willing to part with his investment in order to realise his money. It is a vicious circle. Presumably the man investing in Roman coins also seeks to enjoy his investment and Roman coins provide that enjoyment. Will he so readily part when he needs his capital? My advice is to treat investment potential as an unexpected bonus from the hobby. Speculation is an area for a man with time, capital and the stamina not to cry out when badly stung.

In fact, investment is very much to the rear of most numismatists' minds. Is the collector then simply a jackdaw, accumulating as long as the coin is old? If he follows certain ground rules he need not veer over to this other extreme. He must keep his collecting in perspective. It must not encroach on the family budget. Family holidays should not centre each year around some dismal township where there happens to be a coin dealer. He needs to be able to say 'No' when he'd like to say 'Yes', when material is beyond his pocket. If he can reject coins as being a waste of money, however old and Roman they may be, because they are of poor quality, then he is a discerning collector in control of his addiction.

If a man spends £25 on a hundred very worn coins, the thrill of history in sheer bulk quickly evaporates when he finds that he could have bought a fine specimen of a single coin for the same amount. It is hard to sell bad material. This is not to say there are not bargains among cheap and worn coins. The blank disc showing clearly a miniature countermark which once gave it a new lease of life is a splendid piece of history as well as a survivor over two millennia – perhaps worth just a little respect on those grounds alone (see Fig. 101b).

On his limited purse the small-time collector may envy the petro-dollar connoisseur, the investor with capital or the dealer up to his knees in the flow of circulating Roman coins. Yet the budget collector still has the thrill (and the weariness) of the chase as compensation, the find on the rummage tray which has escaped notice, the bargain at low price which the dealer cannot be bothered to research. He may catch a valuable coin at the end of the runway before it takes off above his purse. Sometimes a simple toothbrush and soap can remove the grime which made a coin appear worn: bought for £2 it might double its price after simple harmless cleaning (Fig. 7).

Such a collector is not a dealer with red plush case and capital invested. On the other hand he might try to make his hobby pay for itself. Poor worn items will not easily re-sell. He may be stuck with them. Occasionally a coin may realise a modest increase, once the collector has done some detective work. It is precisely this knowledge and research which is being paid for in the profit. We pay a dealer for his expert knowledge and efforts as well as his guarantee – in an ideal world. Unwanted specimens might be advertised generally – as novel presents, jewellery ideas or for framing and in this way beginners and

7. *As*, Trajan, *c.* AD 116, with title **Parthicus**; trophies probably indicate the annexation of Armenia and Mesopotamia (£2, 1980).

even non-collectors can enjoy them. They have served the collector's purpose, which is enjoyment and learning; he sells them to realise at least a little of his money back and if lucky he can then go on to buy something better. An £18 *denarius* of Trajan (Fig. 8) is a good return for seven or eight fairly worn *sestertii* which have cost £2 each over a year or two. Obviously no one can retire and live from proceeds like these!

8. *Denarius*, Trajan, after AD 112, depicting Genius. Note stresscracks and striations produced by the striking (£18, 1979).

One experience of buying and selling

By way of illustration, let me share the experience of a coin fair. I stand on the steps of the Town Hall waiting for the fair to open. Dealers pass with cases, calculators and a certain careworn look. They have a preview before the public is admitted. I feel distinctly an amateur. I have a little accumulated knowledge (essential in the tick-tack atmosphere of a coin fair) and a couple of unwanted Roman bronzes in my pocket. A dog-eared little notebook at home records when, where and how much I have paid for each of my coins. I bought these two a year ago – a small Corinthian bronze of Livia for £5 and a worn copper of Germanicus for pence from some tray. 'Damage' on Livia's cheek turns out under the glass to be a minute swastika, a traditional mintmark, counterstruck for some unknown reason.

Once inside the fair I am offered £12 for the Livia and £1 for the copper. Excitement mounts because in the same dealer's tray is a *sestertius* of Trajan in clear detail showing a Dacian prisoner and trophy (Fig. 9). It is priced at £15. I have indicated that I would like it, so the offer is more forthcoming as a part-exchange. Firstly, however, I tour the other stalls to see about comparable offers. One dealer dismisses them as 'rubbish' while another tells me that he always steers clear of Roman. I return, hand over both coins plus £2 (conveniently forgetting the £5.50 paid a year ago!) and come away delighted with the *sestertius*. Both parties are content that little cash has actually changed hands in the deal.

9. *Sestertius*, Trajan, *c.* AD 103–12. **DAC(ia) CAP (ta)** is worn away from the exergue. Trajan's Column in Rome also marked the Dacian campaign. The odd placing of **SC** hints at more than one engraver at work.

Before going I look again round the stalls, noting prices but also looking more carefully at rummage boxes marked from 10 pence to £2. I also barter, rarely accepting the stated price – it is not a liberty. Many a bargain is missed in these boxes, even after expert sifting. There are 'investment' bargains such as the neglected Tsarist small silver. There are pure 'interest' bargains such as the yellow French coins of the days of the Terror: they are made from melted church and

convent bells and are worth a few pence as a teaching aid – for their
'chime' when suspended and struck. I have no capital to lose or stock
to turn over. My bread and butter does not hang on the day. I have
no security worries, ledgers to balance or even a taxman to correspond
with. Perhaps in a coin fair the budget numismatist may be the better
off after all.

In fact, there is something of the investor, accumulator, treasure
hunter, dealer (and budding shark) in every collector. The coin and
the situation brings each to the surface as required. The important
factor is the enjoyment of the whole process of collecting. If the hobby
starts to make the collector unhappy and take over his life, then it is
no longer a hobby but a hoarding obsession – and time he sold up.
After all, we only keep a collection for a time. Someone else eventually
disperses it. It also helps keep a perspective on the whole thing when
we remember that with all the money and time in the world, even the
most priceless collection has its gaps, no less than Diogenes' tub.

Figures and comments in this book will show that billions of coins
flooded the Roman world for hundreds of years. The Roman coin is
common and this is still not generally known. There are infinitely more

10. *Denarii*, Vitellius, July–December AD 69, Rome. Earlier coins from his
Rhine base read **IMP GERM**; he took the title **Augustus** on entering Rome
but refused **Caesar** altogether. (a) The raven, dolphin and tripod bowl, symbols of Delphic Apollo and badge for the College of Fifteen Priests (**XV VIR
SAC**) of which Vitellius was a member. He and they were notorious for their
gluttony (£30.00, 1980). (b) His face shows its true lines on this EF *denarius*
(£1,400, 1981).

available than there were Dinky toys ever manufactured. Compared with the really exclusive areas of collecting such as Japanese netsuke, the field is wide open. In the early Empire an educated slave could cost half a million *sestertii*; the Emperor Vitellius alone spent nine hundred million *sestertii* in a few months – admittedly, a reckoning unit rather than a coin (Fig. 10). There were enough coins for them. There are more than enough for that growing but still relatively small band who now collect what the Romans at least no longer need.

Why collect?

The collecting instinct is an old form of addiction. In the days of Hadrian, Juvenal went as far as to put into poetry his contemptuous pity for the hoarder. Augustus collected fossils. According to Pliny Senior the Romans themselves collected Roman coins. In today's world of drug and solvent addiction my pupils sometimes ask me (in jest) if I go as far as to 'sniff' my coins. I reply (seriously) that I do and there is good reason for it. What has it lain in? What has been used to clean it? Silver smells while inert gold does not. Their faces suggest that their worst fears are all but confirmed.

Roman coins are tangible. The fingertip can read them as well as the eye. They are survivors over an immense period of time. In some cases they are works of art in miniature which everyone can own. Scholars even have reason to believe that some die-cutters were also highly skilled gem-cutters (see Fig. 92). Direct links have been found between certain intaglio-cut gems and coin dies. The skills are closely akin. In other less artistic cases the coins are still a mass of detail once we learn to interpret their official (and unofficial) markings. They are also part of our heritage, directly in Britain as a former Roman colony and more generally as part of the source of much of the world's language, culture and religious traditions.

They are personal items. The fact that they are not quite round is due to hand-striking at the mint. Like the lady's beauty-spot, the imperfection which shows up the rest of the good looks, the flaws and pancaked flans arouse tantalising questions (Fig. 11). They are not machine-made, therefore not quite anonymous. They reveal the heights and depths of human quality control. Who struck it? Who passed it? What sort of day was it? What time of day or week? The questions are not idle. When buying an Eastern-bloc car I was advised to work out from the engine and chassis numbers what time of month the car was made. There is a danger that it might be a hastily finished product, part of the race to meet quota deadlines before the end of the month. A car made at the beginning may have had a little more leisurely care expended on it. Was there just such a human parallel in the mint shops of the Empire?

11. *Quadrantes*, Gaius 'Caligula' and Claudius (see Fig. 14). (a) Marks tax remission; the first dates from AD 40, the second, cut by a different die-sinker, is dated AD 41 – 'Caligula' was assassinated in January AD 41. (b) Claudius issued the corn-measure coin in AD 41 and the hand holding scales in the following year, possibly marking coin reforms (18 mm. Rough and without portraits, hence between £1 and £4, 1980).

Unlike the collector of modern coins, the Roman collector does not have to worry about bag scratches and finger marks. Twenty centuries of these and every other conceivable mark has brought them to the point where the scratches themselves can be of historical interest. (There is no need to add to them. The Aldershot drill-sergeant's advice for shining boots also applies to handling coins: 'Don't paw them with sweaty fingers or breathe on them after eating chips!')

Sitting at a desk the coin-archaeologist can 'read' his metal pieces and work out much of their story in the same way as the gumbooted field-worker reads the stones and the furrows. Roman coins bring out the detective. For years I have had a coin of Jewish Samaria, the battered product of a rummage tray (Fig. 12). One day I found, among the pittings and digs of a very bad surface, the mark of the famous Legion X *Fretensis*. This legion boasted Jerusalem and Masada among its battle honours before settling down to garrison Palestine (see Ch. VII). The family smiled tolerantly and saw nothing. Friends were kind. A photographer enlarged pictures of it to giant proportions and still saw nothing – he was a born diplomat. At last, someone else saw the **(L)X F** and I felt that my name was cleared. Even the family now admit – or claim – they can see it too. A caution is necessary: one such find can lead to seeing marks of *all* Rome's army listed legions on cor-

12. *Ae 24 mm*, Domitian and (Marcus) Agrippa II, AD 87, Flavia Neapolis (Nablus), Samaria. Countermarked vertically on the neck. Legion X *Fretensis* had a detachment quartered in this veteran *colonia* near the ruined Biblical Shechem. The Paymaster was evidently short of Imperia coin that year. Reverse reads in Greek **FLAVI(a) NEAPOL(is) SAM(ariae) AGR(ippae) L 31** (£1, 1978).

roded surfaces of any kind. Wishful thinking bordering on the mirage is a hazard of coin collecting.

Coins provide a therapy like that of a good book. After a day spent working with people, inanimate objects stay in line, don't create problems and don't answer back. They also open up whole new areas of knowledge. To me the Financial Index means little. Inflation still takes considerable understanding in an age of international finance and political economics. Put in terms of debased metal, token taking over from real value, trimming, plating, alloying and the eventual disappearance of key denominations altogether, I can begin to grasp it. This in turn leads to understanding the effects of inflation, such as a vast surplus of small coinage, the hoarding instinct and sheer fear arising from insecurity as 'the *denarius* in your pocket' loses value overnight.

Coins also take the collector into the troubled world of rebellion, to the loneliness and comradeship of military tours of duty and into the mind of the looter, often no more than a simple soldier 'liberating' an object with no obvious owner.

The art of emotional and theatrical propaganda was only inherited by Goebbels, not invented by him. Coins of the Roman world offer an insight into the manipulation of people, the false blanket headline, the bogus proclamations of confidence in a failing currency and the deifying of rulers who were all too human and flawed. In the same way as I gazed fascinated as a child at the regimented parting and firmly chiselled profile of George VI on his pennies, the ancients too must have mused over Nero's wrestler's chin, Vespasian's military jawline and Nerva's eagle nose.

If a collector is drawn by the fascination of 'Whose hands once touched this coin?' he might also tempt his imagination further with the equally tantalising question, 'Where did this metal come from?' Much silver of the house of Constantine came from the melting of pagan temple vessels after the official change in religion. Some at least of the Carausian bronze may have come from the melting of household utensils as well as old coinage in a sort of third-century British 'Spitfire Fund'. Many silver *denarii* of the Flavians started their lives either in Britain's lead mines or in the plate looted from Judea in AD 70. The leaden Jewish *prutah* (see Fig. 85) may well have come from household pipes or the flashing of a roof in a last desperate gesture of normality by the besieged rebel garrison of Jerusalem. The questions arising from 'reading' the Roman coin are endless. These are what draw and fascinate the collector.

II

THE ROMAN COIN – A TOUGH SURVIVOR

> When you go on a night journey, though you may only
> have a few small treasures with you, you'll take every stir-
> ring shadow, each moonlit reed for a sound or cudgel, but
> the empty-handed traveller whistles his way past any
> highwayman.
>
> Juvenal, *Satire X, c.* AD 125

The purpose

To our youngest son Roman coins are 'old moneys'. This withering
description, usually uttered when trying to drag me from coinshop to
toyshop, has a five-year-old's uncanny accuracy. They are simply long
discontinued currency. Currency is a convenient means of exchange
and payment, accepted by a population and stamped with its government's guarantee. The artistic forms of the Roman state stamp are
what draw collectors.

'Roman' for coin purposes covers **Republican** down to about 50 BC,
then **Imperatorial** down to the battle of Actium in 31 BC and **Imperial**
from that date to the last emperor in the West in AD 476. This can, of
course, be extended to include the surviving 'new Rome' at Constantinople, known by its older Greek name of Byzantium. The Tsarist
eagle on the vodka bottles also reminds us that there was even a 'third
Rome', now better known as Moscow, where the Grand Duke married
a Byzantine princess just after the fall of Constantinople in AD 1453.

The artwork served more purposes than just guaranteeing bullion.
The coin was a miniature newspaper passing through many hands, a
political broadcast in braille. Along with the great carved monuments
it was one of the few ancient mass media. The literate could read its
'headline' on the reverse and its 'proprietor's' claims on the obverse
titles. Strong portraits and a telling reverse evoked some sort of feeling
in everyone. In AD 70, mints across the Roman world began 'telegraph-
ing' the news of the end of the Jewish Revolt while the ash in Jerusalem
was still warm and several years before the final mopping-up operations in the Judean desert were complete. The 'headline' of that particular issue – **Iudaea Capta!** – has become a numismatic legend (Fig.
13). Like modern newspaper copy, coin dies must have been prepared

13. *Sestertii*, Vespasian, AD 69–79. Different 'headlines' declare **Peace !** (a) Male and female Jewish prisoners with surrendered weapons under Judean palm tree, **Iudaea Capta !** (b) Pax with olive branch and horn of prosperity, **Pax Augusti !** (c) Pax lights a bonfire of weapons in front of victory column, **Pax Augusti!** (Several hundred pounds each in auction, 1981, due to condition, design and popularity of the earlier *sestertius*).

in anticipation of the outcome and taken off the shelf for immediate production once news came through.

Half Per Cent Tax Scrapped! proclaim 'Caligula's' smallest bronzes (Fig. 14a) but there is no such publicity for the other taxes he imposed. A year later, Claudius announced money and standards reforms on his own tiny *quadrantes* (Fig. 14b). Nerva made the most of a sixteen-month reign with **Fraud in Jewish Tax Checked!** and **Imperial Transport Tax in Italy Abolished!** (Fig. 15). In wishful thinking he portrayed the combined services standard behind clasped hands, **The Support of the Forces!**, an appeal which the soldier-Emperors Trajan and Hadrian turned into a reality. 'Headlines' on their coins read like telexed military communiqués: **Dacians Put Down! Armenia and Mesopotamia Under Roman Control! Discipline in the Army!** (this along with variations naming eleven different Army groups); **The Man Who Put Spain/Gaul/Africa/The Whole World Back on its Feet!** (Figs. 16, 17)

A common but moving set of issues marks the love of Antoninus Pius for his wife and posthumously for her memory − **Faustina Always!** (Fig. 18). The list is endless. Designers at the Roman mint seem to have had the services of caption and headline writers to match any employed by a newspaper or commercial advertiser today.

14. *Quadrantes*, Gaius 'Caligula' and Claudius, (see Fig. 11.) (a) 'Caligula', AD 40. **RCC** may mean **Remissa Ducentesima**, abolition of the half per cent defence tax on sales. A cap of liberty is shown. (b) Claudius, AD 42. **PNR** may mean **Ponderum Norma Restituta**, weights and measures norms restored; more attractively for collectors, it may indicate **Pondus Nummorum Restitutum**, coin weight restored, apparently after reductions by Gaius (Superb condition sold them for £50 and £35 respectively in 1981).

15. *Sestertii*, Nerva, AD 96–8. (a) The end of the scandal whereby anyone even said to be Jewish had to pay the punitive tax on Jews (see Ch. VII). (b) Abolition of tax imposed on Italians for the Imperial Courier Service – mules graze, presumably in a rest paddock at a staging post. (c) clasped hands and the insignia of army and navy (galley beak below military standard) imply backing for Nerva (In this condition, several hundred pounds each at auction, 1982).

16. *Sestertii*, Trajan, AD 98–117. Both (a) and (c) proclaim his victory over the Dacians and the securing of the Danube frontier while (b) shows Armenia and the two rivers, Tigris and Euphrates, at Trajan's feet (each sold for about £150, 1981).

17. *Sestertii*, Hadrian, AD 117–38. (a) Marks his good government of **Gaul**. (b) **Cappadocia** with a model of the sacred Mount Argaeus and a military standard marks his work on the Asia Minor frontier. (c) One of a series marking his inspection of frontier garrisons, in this case the **Dacian** legions (auction estimate in 1982 for (a) and (b), £280 and £180 respectively; (c) cost the collector £10, 1980).

18. *Sestertii*, posthumous of Faustina Senior, after AD 141. (a) Veiled and deified, depicted on the reverse as **Mother of the Army Camps!** the heavenly protector of the legions. (b) Veiled and deified, **Eternity !** (Auction estimates £450 and £200 respectively, 1982. Worn sestertii of Faustina are quite common and generally cheap, being the survivors of a volume production. See Fig. 67c).

Headline events cannot be made to happen to order. More frequently general fallback themes appear such as **Justice Restored!** after Domitian's reign of terror, or **Peace!** after the four rival Emperors of AD 68–9 **Liberty!** was understandable on coins of Claudius and Galba immediately following the megalomaniacs 'Caligula' and Nero. On the coins of the third-century rebel Carausius, a new mark announced a mint in London, thereby setting a seal of respectability and viability on his rebel island empire and its capital (see Fig. 144). Sometimes the news bordered more on wishful thinking. Despite his independence, Carausius minted his titles and even his bust in the plural along with those of the legitimate rulers on the Continent. Galba, Otho and Vitellius during the 'Year of the Four' broadcast **Peace!** and their titles on the coinage, but this was more manifesto than reality. When Vespasian depicted his sons in handshaking harmony, it hinted as much at his misgivings as at his confidence in their compatibility. When Titus died after an indecently short reign, rumour pointed to Domitian as the poisoner.

News, hopes, assurances and warnings all feature on Imperial reverses. Today we might call it propaganda. Where personal power was at a peak, as under Nero, propaganda became self-glorification. Nero was shown as Apollo playing the lyre (Fig. 19), in triumph as a general and on manoeuvres as a seasoned cavalryman (Fig. 20). Elagabalus vaunted his priestly dignities to the point of provoking nausea while Domitian took credit for minor frontier wars in the style and wording of his father and brother's Judean commemoratives (Fig. 21). **Germans Defeated!** (see Fig. 104), and other victory issues awoke recent echoes of greater events: Domitian needed to compensate an ego bruised by his exclusion from the family victory over the Jews and other Imperial rivals. The balmier days of the Republic had set a quiet precedent for all this later vainglory. Republican *denarii* read like a Debrett's of Roman society, showing nearly two hundred family 'achievements' from the annual moneyers in office.

19. *Asses*, Nero, *c.* AD 66. Nero dressed as the god of music strums a lyre. Nero did sing in the Olympics of AD 66 – possibly one origin of the saying that he 'fiddled while Rome burned'. Suetonius notes this coin as the peak of vanity (*nummum percussit*). (a) Experimental *as* in orichalcum; note the denomination **I** in the exergue (23 mm). (b) Standard copper *as*, badly worn, bought for pence from a rummage tray, 1978 (28 mm).

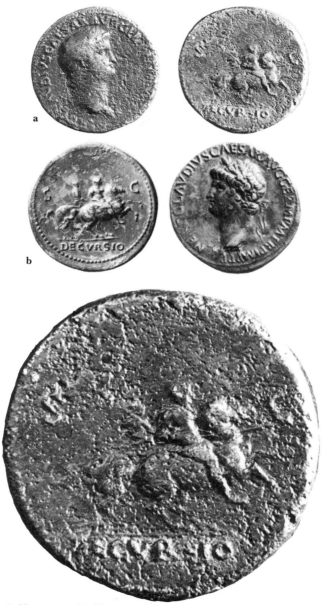

20. *Sestertii*, Nero, *c.* AD 65. Nero as a lancer on manoeuvres (**decursio**) accompanied by adjutant with standard. (a) The worn copy is enlarged to show the miniature portrait of the rider; obverse shows how the design-cutter left a band of metal round the die circumference for the legend-cutter (£25, 1981). (b) This superb version would be priced at around £500 in 1982.

21. *Sestertii* and *dupondius*, Domitian, AD 81–96. (a) Domitian receives the loyalty of the army's representatives. (b) Domitian is crowned by the goddess of
Victory after the German campaigns. (c) Victory adorns a trophy of the German wars. (a) and (b) in this condition, several hundred pounds each at auction, 1982; (c) fairly worn yet distinct, £2, 1980).

Often – but by no means always – the coins were works of art. Nero
is thought to have imported skilled Greek die-cutters and designers for
his voluminous coinage of AD 64 onwards. From the time of Augustus,
portrait and reverse design had grown increasingly more lifelike. Nero's
reign set a standard which continued throughout the Flavian period
well into the next century. The skill of the original craftsmen was either
continually reinforced with new arrivals or at least handed on through
a rigorous school of apprenticeship. Some of the portraits from Nero
to Hadrian, particularly where heavy striking shows high relief at its
best, are miniature classical sculptures (Fig. 22).

With a few magnificent exceptions the high relief sinks lower during
the second and third centuries as the dies grow shallower. Wooden
features and crude, almost Gothic lettering in the third century prepare
us for the stylised and impersonal portraits of the house of Constantine
(Fig. 23). Perhaps the last Roman attempts at realism are the finer
coins of the London and 'Fleet' mints under Carausius and Allectus.
Their die-cutters may have come in from the Continent, seeing a new
world of opportunity opening up in this North Sea island. They would
also be well out of the way of the Eastern influences which were beginning to change the traditional face of Roman art.

22. *Dupondius*, Vespasian, AD 76. Bold relief and the new radiate crown for the *dupondius* are mated with an older reverse die, Victory with shield inscribed **S(enatus) P(opulus) Q(ue) R(omanus)**. The so-called 'globe' at the tip of the neck is a legend-stop, the mark of a western mint (Lyons?) (£14, 1980).

23. *Ae 3*, (possibly known as *centenionalis*) and reduced *follis*, Constantine I, AD 307–37. The symbols and dress of office take priority over realistic portrait and even anatomical accuracy! Though it is doubtful that Constantine ever became a Christian, he was titled 'Defender of the Church' and hailed as 'The Thirteenth Apostle' (£1, 1979 and £45, 1981 respectively).

Where some coins have been struck more carefully than others, with especially fine dies and on precisely circular flans, there is always the possibility that we are handling commemorative pieces like the British crowns. Double-thickness flans which are sometimes found could, in some cases at least, be deliberate *piedforts* – presentation mementos of a volume striking – currency certainly, but hardly meant for spending. A grey and ill-defined border separates the coin from the commemorative medallion: the latter are often exact multiples of *denarii* or *aurei*.

It is worth noting that coins were also used as items of personal decoration. The body was almost as safe a bank as the earth, certainly more interesting. Pierced, mounted and usually the more readily affordable silver, coins were worn on headdress, ears and neck. The fact that a coin has a jewellery mark should not detract from it – although fortunately for collectors it does so and greatly reduces the price. There is added interest in reading the wear-marks and trying to work out, for instance, how long it was used as an ornament (see Fig. 115). When two *denarii* of a couple such as Severus and Julia Domna are found pierced in the same spot, it makes an attractive guess that here was once a pair of pendent earrings. Such coins are sometimes in good condition (apart from the hole) as they have tended to escape the wear and tear inflicted by circulation.

The metals

Bronze was the basic metal of exchange in early Rome. Copper, its chief component, took its name from the productive mines of the island of Cyprus. When, under the Empire, zinc was added to copper to create *orichalcum* ('mountain copper'), the middle denominations of coin took on a richness somewhere between gold and brass. In fact, Pliny Senior accepted the word as being *aurichalcum* ('golden copper'). Silver was used throughout all periods of Roman coining although with recurrent debasement and attempts at restoration of standards.

With inflation, increasing amounts of base metal were added to the silver until late in the third century silver disappeared altogether, making only a brief, insular and illegal comeback in Britain under Carausius and Allectus (AD 287–96). Presumably trading confidence and the loyalty of their legions were best secured by the finest standard of payment. Britain's silver mines also afforded the opportunity. In the second and third centuries zinc also disappeared from the large bronze and the coins became darker as more tin and even lead took its place. In fact it shows up rather attractively in the multicoloured patina of the last issues of *sestertii* (see p. 60). Even copper had lost its red purity by the early second century. Gold is beyond the scope of this book and of most readers' purses. Naturally it formed the highest denominations of both Republic and Empire, retaining its fineness if not its weight.

The denominations

(See also The Roman denominations on p. 168) A stamped lump (*pondus*) of bronze (*aes*) soon developed into a large disc or pound (*libra pondo*) of set weight and stamped rather as we know a coin. In Rome this coin (*aes/as*) in diminishing sizes remained the standard low denomination for 500 years. Sometime in the third century BC the

24. *Denarii*, Republic. (a) 134 BC, C. Aburius Geminus moneyer; head of Roma with the denomination mark beneath her chin (£90, 1981). (b) 64 BC, L. Roscius Fabatus moneyer; Juno Sospita, heavenly guardian of childbirth and an apparently pregnant woman feeding a snake, presumably that of the health god Aesclepius. Serrated as a reassurance against plating (£320, 1981).

Republic produced silver coins. They were Greek in style and were based on the southern Italian Greek *drachma*. On the latest evidence these were superseded just before 200 BC by the silver piece-of-ten-asses (*denarius*) (Fig. 24). It had silver subdivisions, the piece-of-five-asses (*quinarius*) and the piece-of-two-and-a-half-asses (*sestertius*). In bronze there was a two-pounder or double-*as* (*dupondius*), the basic *as* and its several subunits which included the half-*as* (*semis*) and quarter-*as* (*quadrans*). The *as* was an unmistakeably large coin, usually struck with the double head of Janus, sometimes elderly, sometimes youthful, and carrying on its reverse a ship's prow and the simple legend **ROMA** (Fig. 25). It is frequently found on dealers' trays in poor condition.

After about 80 BC bronze disappeared. Silver became the backbone of the later Republican currency.

Octavian as a young triumvir (member of a three-man *junta*) in the provinces, minted large bronzes which took on the old name *sestertius* soon after Caesar's assassination (Fig. 26). Once he was head of state as Augustus he created a *sestertius* together with a *dupondius* in the new metal, orichalcum. Below these were issued a pure copper *as*, a periodic orichalcum *semis* and a bronze, sometimes copper, *quadrans* (Fig. 27). These remained the basic low denomination currency for nearly two centuries. In the second century AD the *quadrans* and *semis* disappeared completely. The *sestertius* suffered both in content and in weight until it too disappeared after the mid-third century (see Figs. 62 and 69). There was a shortlived double-*sestertius* under Trajan Decius and the usurper Postumus (Fig. 28). The smaller *dupondius* and *as* also disappeared with the *sestertius* after suffering similar debasement.

As early as the days of Nero the *denarius* began to lose its bullion fineness. It was progressively alloyed until it bottomed out at about 40 per cent silver in the third century. This later *denarius* tarnishes less easily and tends to have either a grey or a chromelike sheen, quite unlike the moonlustre of fine silver. 'Caracalla' (properly Marcus Aurelius Antoninus) introduced a new coin, named *antoninianus* after

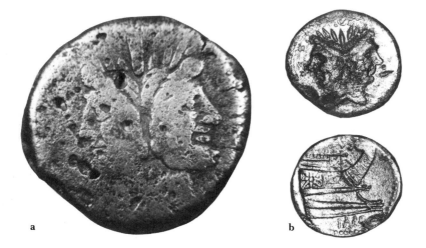

a   b

25. *Asses*, Republican and Imperatorial. (a) Late second century BC, ounce weight, typical of the worn condition of many such coins found on dealers' trays; double head of Janus and denomination mark **I**. January and Janitor are derived from this name; two heads indicate that beginnings and entrances also serve as ends and exits (32 mm. £1, 1979) (b) Sextus Magnus Pius Pompey, *c.* 43 BC, Sicily. Janus carries the features of the late Pompey the Great and the galley reverse carries the son's title **PIUS IMP** in place of the traditional **ROMA**. (30 mm. £150, 1980).

26. *Sestertius*, Octavian, *c.* 36 BC, Italy. Apparently the first *sestertius* in base metal which heralded the orichalcum coin of a decade later. Octavian is described **DIVI F(ilius)** while his adoptive father is now deified, **DIVUS IULIUS** (£30, 1981).

27. *As*, Augustus, 7 BC, M. Maecilius Tullus moneyer (see also Figs 50 and 88) (£65, 1981).

28. *Double sestertius*, Trajan Decius, AD 249–51. Part of an attempt to restabilise an inflating currency. (a) Is not only rare but in unusually magnificent condition, hence sold for £1,900, 1981. (b) While still equally infrequently encountered, this more worn version would cost the collector around £200, 1982.

himself and probably worth two *denarii* (Fig. 29a). Like the *dupondius* and the later shortlived double-*sestertius*, it was a 'radiate' – its obverse bust was crowned with the sun's rays. A female bust, however, was half-framed from below by the crescent moon (Fig. 29b). This sun-crown may have been Imperial Rome's only lasting denominational mark on the coinage, denoting even to the unlettered that the coin was double the value of a similar coin carrying only the laurel-crown. By the time of the Flavians it was standard on the *dupondius*, although it is less easily understood when found on occasional gold of Domitian and on Trajan's orichalcum *asses* and *semisses* (Fig. 30).

29. *Antoniniani*, 'Caracalla', Julia Domna and Balbinus, *c.* AD 215 and AD 238. (a) Shows the new coin in superb condition, proclaiming the radiate-crowned 'Caracalla' as the sun god in chariot while (b) compliments his mother, Julia Domna, as the reflective moon goddess, also in chariot. (c) Balbinus' more sober restoration showing his hand clasped in that of his co-Emperor, Pupienus. The coin soon lost its 50 per cent silver fineness, eventually collapsing as low as 1 per cent (the collector would pay well over £100 for these *antoniniani* in such condition in 1982).

30. *Dupondius* and 'radiate' *as*, Trajan, AD 98–117. (a) Was by this time a standard orichalcum 'radiate' or double-*as*. (b) It is less clear why the *semis* and *as* were also issued as 'radiates' save to distinguish them from older standard issues; perhaps the intention was to dispense with copper-bronze altogether (£1 and £2 respectively, 1982).

Republican bronze had long carried symbols for the *as, semis* and other subdivisions in the form of an **I**, an **S** and an appropriate number of dots respectively. Silver, too, for some time under the Republic had carried the numerals **X** and **V** on the *denarius* and *quinarius*. Nero experimented with the coins for four years, reintroducing the symbols **II**, **I** and **S** on some of his *dupondii, asses* and *semisses* (Fig. 31); the dots on some of his *quadrantes* may also be significant. Although the *sestertius* had its own distinguishing mark, **IIS**, it never appeared on the coins; it is, however, found on many inscriptions, used for centuries as a reckoning unit of finance (Fig. 32).

a   b

31. *Semisses*, Nero, AD 65. These mark the second of the Five-Yearly Neronian Games; the adjudicator's table carries a balloting urn and a prizewinner's crown. (a) Struck at a western mint, (?Lyons) without denomination mark (£2, 1979). (b) Struck in Rome with the additional mark **S**. (£130, 1981).

32. Tomb inscription of the Supsifanii family, seventh mile of the Via Appia south of Rome; the monument cost '27,500 sestertii' and the sign **IIS** is crossed by a connecting line to distinguish its meaning.

By about AD 270 the *antoninianus* had displaced the *denarius* altogether and had itself degenerated into a base coin with a shoddy 'pickled' surface and the tiniest trace of silver. Even miniature *antoniniani* known as 'radiate minims' and only 5 mm in diameter passed as legal tender in this depressing period. English courts now refuse to class later *antoniniani* as treasure trove, no matter the size of the find. Justice may be blindfolded but she still knows the feel of purely notional silver (Fig. 33).

Another attempt to renew the coinage took place at the start of the fourth century AD (see Appendix IV). The *denarius* reappeared as the *argenteus* and a large silver-washed billon or base silver coin recalled the older large bronze of more stable times. This latter is conventionally known as the *follis* or 'purse money', from the Latin word for a leather money-bag. Its real name is unknown (Fig. 34). The large coin quickly declined in size although the silver wash remained for some time and can still be found in traces on many reduced or quarter-size *folles* of *c* AD 313 onwards. The rest of the fourth century saw numerous brief attempts to return to a sound silver and bronze currency.

33. *Antoniniani* of (a–e) Gordian III, Philip, Valerian, Gallienus and Tacitus. The declining fineness of the coin could not be disguised by plating or 'pickling'. In the 'Gallic Empire' of Britain, Gaul and Germany, the coin varied in standard and declined to virtual bronze under Tetricus I. A shortage of coin and confidence in coin prompted the 'radiate minim' *c.* AD 270 enlarged in (f) from 5 mm, the flan probably made from quarterings of other base *antoniniani* (coins (a)–(e) are in EF condition. In lesser grades *antoniniani* can be bought quite cheaply; (f) £0.50, 1975).

The *siliqua* (literally a small weight, a bean or a pod!) superseded the *argenteus*. The *centenionalis* and for a short time the handsome large bronzes of Julian were efforts to make bronze respectable (Fig. 35). Even in this world of constantly changing denominations and anony-

34. *Folles*, Diocletian and Galerius. (a) London *c.* AD 300, no mintmark (£40, 1982). (b) Section **3, ALE(xandria) mint**, Galerius as Caesar, AD 293–305. Much of the plating survives on the billon core (*c.* £20, 1982). Worn large *folles* are relatively plentiful and cheap, but not in this condition.

mous bronzes, the human instinct to use older familiar terms in order to soothe the pain and insecurity of changing times was evident. In fact so much did they stick to older denominational terms for reckoning that we know hardly any of the proper denominational names from the fourth century. Nothing is new under the sun! In England they still pay some professional bills in guineas, speak of shillings and strike crowns for special occasions. There is now no technical place for any of them in the English currency and the last guinea was issued in 1813!

The survivors

Fourth-century Romans still nostalgic for their *denarii* would be pleased that some of their treasured coin names have lingered down as far as the twentieth century. They must have resisted coinage reforms as much as the English resisted decimalisation, at least mentally. The *denarius*, through the medieval European *denier*, is still echoed in the Jugoslav *dinar*, *d* of the old English penny (once silver and the size of a *denarius*), and the Italian word for money in general, *denaro*. The

35. Restored *folles*, Julian II, AD 361–3, (usually called *Ae 1.*) The bull which earned jeers from the people of Antioch may be that of the Egyptian god, Apis, or more simply it may be Julian's birthsign and a symbol of his strong government. The twin stars are Castor and Pollux, Rome's protectors. Julian was later dubbed 'Apostate' because he supported pagan virtues, blaming official Christianity for sapping Rome's strength. Tradition has his dying words, 'You've won, Galilean'. (a) **M(oneta) SIRM(ium)**. (b) Section **2, ANT(ioch) mint**. (£200 and £300 respectively, 1981. Collectors can obtain low-quality versions for much less).

Republican *libra* has survived in our abbreviation for weight, *lb*, the currency symbol £, the *litre* and of course in the Italian *lira*. *Pondo* is still preserved most obviously in the word *pound* and lightly camouflaged in the words *ponderous* and *expenditure*. Perhaps most surprising of all is the smallest coin of the Republic, the *uncia* or one-twelfth *as* which continues in the form of our tinier measurements, the *inch* and the *ounce*.

Even more tangible than their ghosted names, the coins themselves are still with us. One historian has estimated that the 30,000 troops forming Britain's island garrison, in AD 150 alone must have received payment that year of nearly seven million *denarii*. The island was occupied for nearly four hundred years. Add the influx of private money, income from trade and civil administrative expenses. Britain was but one of many provinces. Rome authorised coinage over seven hundred years (add another thousand to that if you include Byzantine!). By the fourth century AD two dozen official state mints operated in the Empire. Before that, other Imperial mints and innumerable local mints had been pouring out coinage. This is still not taking into account the moneyers' dens which tried to fill gaps in circulating small change with their volume production of 'barbarous' copies. Even allowing for the failure of currency supplies towards the end of the Western Empire and allowing for increased barter and payment in kind, we must still be dealing with a total of millions upon millions of Roman coins.

Of course, many were recalled and melted. Many have not been found. The fact remains that many have. Coins do not burn, tear or suffer worm; they do not take up much space – to the grateful relief of the families of collectors. They do get brittle; they do corrode beyond recognition and break in hostile environments. 'That's no coin – that's shrapnel!' said a friend scornfully of one *antoninianus* fresh out of the ground (Fig. 36).

If then there are so many Roman coins available, where have they been all this time and where do they come from now? It is first of all necessary to ask where have England's missing sixpences and large pennies all gone, because they did not all go back for redemption. It is then worth noting the current attitude to the half-new-penny, that celebrated fraction inside a decimal system. When dropped it goes unnoticed. Brown bronze then sits camouflaged on dark ground, growing darker and all the less visible for its size. Similarly, the presence in the earth and on dealers' trays of so many thousands of small later Roman bronze, nameless save for their descending order of size (*Ae* 1–4), is not really surprising. 'The gutters of Britain,' said a member of the House of Lords in 1982, 'are scattered with horrible tiny coins, the half pennies, because people can not be bothered to pick them up. This must be costing Britain a fortune.' He could just as well have been speaking in AD 350.

The conditions in which a coin has lain will save or destroy it. Clay and silt tend to preserve. 'Found on the bed of the Tiber' (or Rhone, or Thames, or Garigliano) is a note sometimes appended to the finest of coins in an auction (Fig. 37). They are also preserved pressed into the cement of a tomb, acting as both a datemark and the 'ferryman's fee'. Those lying near the surface of open farmland tend to have suffered; acidic and salty soil will encourage corrosion. I know one field-walker who picks up on average over one hundred coins a year while exercising his dogs on a former Roman district of Wiltshire; all are found lying exposed on the topsoil and almost all of them are in poor condition. Modern fertilisers which reach deep into the soil with new chemicals are now known to speed 'coin rot'. On examination most coins of bronze will show the effects of soil corrosion – in many cases the soil itself still clings in the crevices of the design. Under that soil

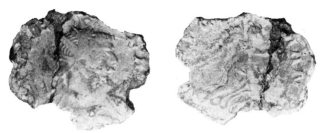

36. *Antoninianus*, Gallienus, AD 253–68, (broken to test for plate?). Found on surface by field walker in England. **Victoria Germanica**.

37. *Dupondius*, Nero, *c.* AD 65, Western mint (Lyons?). Found 'as minted' with lustre, preserved in the clay bed of the Garigliano, Italy A common coin, its rare condition explains the price of £2,500 paid in 1981.

or fleck of grit, unless it is grime from years above ground, there is often irreversible damage. Even the most careful of cleaning may well not reveal the original surface intact.

Hoards

Hoards, both ancient and modern and at times running into thousands of coins, keep the market well fed. In Britain alone over 1,400 recorded caches of Roman coin have been unearthed. The modern 'hoards' are in fact collections, constantly being broken up and sold. The condition of the ancient ones may be protected by an original container. Often, however, they were already quite worn when secreted (see Fig. 48). They may even be damaged, sometimes fused together by oxidization into the shape of the container such as a bag or a bronze jar (Fig. 38). Fire will also melt and fuse them beyond recognition. Melted silver *denarii* were found under the ash at Pompeii, still clinging together in the shape of a long disintegrated bag. I know of one brickworks which is a Roman site and regularly produces blackened distorted discs, once Imperial *denarii* (Fig. 39, also see Fig. 44). When the Goths sacked Rome in AD 410 they put most great buildings to the torch; bronze

38. Hoard of nearly 2,600 *antoniniani* (Valerian – Carausius) found in concretion in a fluted bronze bowl during housebuilding, Penard, Gower, South Wales, 1966. The latest coins near the top suggest a 'current account' hoard and a stray early *denarius* indicates a hoard buried for its contemporary value at the end of the third century.

39. *Denarius*, Titus, AD 79–81, disfigured by fire. From a kiln site in southern England.

coins fused on to the marble floor by those fires can still be seen in the Basilica Aemiliana in the Forum.

There is a popular picture of the hoarder towards the end of the Empire burying his cache as the din and fire of battle threatened his homestead. It has some truth. Pictish invaders or Saxon pirates may well explain why some never returned for their property. The Mildenhall silver found on a wartime airfield is an example. This is by no means the whole story. In Egypt, for instance, hoards of coins, sometimes in thousands, are found hidden beneath the floors of houses. The rural (or *pagan* – for that is the original meaning of the word) Roman world knew very little deposit banking. In a city it was different. Guarded temples made good safe-deposits – up to a point. Juvenal cites two temples burgled due to lax security measures.

In the country the earth was Nature's ready-made bank, as the lazy servant in the Gospel parable of the pounds well knew. He even wrapped his bullion bar in a napkin so that it could be proved to be a deposit rather than a lost item. If a man went on a journey and had no stewards he would not leave his money in the house; he buried it. On return he might have decided to leave it in that safe place. In a period of economic instability, immense piles of coin were salted away; hoards of 42,000 and 56,000 coins are known from the later third century, in one case weighing over 150 kilograms (Fig. 40). Today some still trust floorboards, wall-safes, chimneys, lofts and even the loosened top few inches of the wallpaper. The earthen pots, glass bottles and even the hollow bone of Roman times are different only in detail.

This leads us to the main reason for hoarding. 'Bad money drives out good.' Dealers today advertise for pre-1947 English silver. Although much of it is still legal tender, it is no longer found in pocket change due simply to its increased metal worth. Nor has the Mint accounted for all of it. Similarly, no one in their right mind would dream of using the gold sovereign as currency with its notional value of £1. Until recent years it was English law that no more than five sovereigns could be held at once, otherwise it amounted to illegal hoarding, withholding scarce gold from a debt-crippled government. Financial crises and hard times, not to mention the taxman's scrutiny, breed hoarders just as effectively and far less dramatically than the shrieks of barbarian raiders. When Aurelian refused to recognise the notional value of the debased *antoniniani* in AD 273, some people simply buried them and waited for him to die. It was a vain gamble: they were eventually completely demonetised.

Soldiers by their very occupation are men who have to travel light. They buried loot on the march, fingers always crossed in the hope that they would live to return along the same road. They did the same with their pay and bounties while on routine tours of duty. Night life and shopping outlets at The Wall must have been strictly low-key, perhaps in sober contrast to life in today's better army bases at home and

40. Portion of the Bath Hoard, 1,800 coins, mostly *antoniniani* of the 'Gallic Emperors', found in the remains of a lead bucket, 1979. Some hoards of this period seem to have been secreted after the attempts of Aurelian and Probus to scrap the 'radiate' altogether. Some hoarders were simply misers, while others 'banked' their savings underground. The whole mass weighed a half-kilogram; cleaned by the method described on p. 180. See also Fig. 65.

abroad. On return home pensions would also be hidden away carefully, just as the modern reservist banks his annual bounty to pay for the family holiday.

The common drainage system reveals less dramatic secrets. I found my first Roman coins in a sewer just below a vertical downspout (Fig. 41). Open any road drain, scour the sump of any well or sewer and the lost bric-à-brac of yesterday comes to the surface. Such strays add up. The most intriguing group I have seen recorded was a small pile of Roman coppers 'from thirty fathoms down a copper mine under an artificial island in a creek of Falmouth harbour'.

Tree roots burst the soil and reveal what was hidden there before the tree. Dogs dig for rabbits and scatter coins. In one case, a 'ghost' led witnesses to a Roman hoard in a piggery! Ploughs go over town, villa and camp sites all over the former Roman Empire once or twice a year. The farmer, like the Italian navvy, keeps a weather-eye open when working on a known historical site. One annually harvested strip near my home is sprinkled with Roman small change, the losses from

41. The contents of a Roman drain sump: (L–R) bone needles, dice and game counters; coins (Figs 4 and 44) from Domitian to Antoninus; flask and lamp, both still smelling of olive oil; cameo stone.

fairs held around a temple shrine in Roman times. Even children playing in the garden produce their trophies: I have been presented with Roman coins dug up by children playing in the soil at home in places as far apart as Oxfordshire and Samaria (Fig. 42). The 1979 excavations in Bath brought up more than 8,000 coins, thrown as offerings to the waters of Sulis Minerva, the Romano-British deity.

The advent of the metal detector has brought still more coins to light and·brought heated controversy in their wake. It has even caused a drop in certain prices as once 'scarce' coins come out of the ground in increasing numbers – those of Carausius and Allectus are an example. Strict laws now control the use of detectors in England. It is to be hoped that the treasure hunter gouging into an historical site (or worse, into a current excavation overnight) is a dying breed. Where detector-owners are members of a responsible club and where archaeologists can overcome a possessive sense of monopoly or a personal desire for fame, both parties can even work together for mutual benefit. If my garden is an unknown Roman site, revealed only by a chance metal-detector find, then a discovery has been made which years of study might never have even suggested and which fertiliser or building may soon destroy.

The problem remains that a coin torn from context is like a page ripped from a good book. In itself it may be interesting but only a

42. *As*, Antoninus Pius, AD 150, which appeared on a gardener's trowel in Italy – a common occurrence in a classical country. Justice is seated, her name almost obliterated in the exergue.

fraction of a much wider story and making less than full sense on its own. This applies to most of the coins encountered by the collector; they will have no pedigree or story attached to them. Take, for example, the clipped *siliquae* (Fig. 43). On the other hand a badly burnt *sestertius* of Antoninus Pius was found just below a thick band of ash (Fig. 44). This, along with others below and above the ash, allowed us to date fairly precisely a great fire in the building above; this in turn matched a fire in that region of the city recorded by chroniclers of the days of Antoninus Pius.

A word of warning may be necessary for the reader. As you walk across a villa site, over a Roman road or along Hadrian's Wall, do not allow your blood-pressure to rise as you dream of sculpted *sestertii* and tarnished silver in the subsoil below your feet. Good money was

43. *Siliquae*, Arcadius (AD 383–408) and his younger brother Honorius (AD 393–423), found in London by the Thames. Clipping suggests that legends mattered little to a semi-literate society, particularly after the Roman withdrawal, but the busts were an accepted assay-mark. The context is lost and the rest of the story behind these mute witnesses to the state of the *diocesis Britanniarum* in AD 410, when Honorius is said to have abandoned Roman claims to Britain (£1 and £12 respectively, 1982).

44. *Sestertii*, Antoninus Pius, AD 138–61. (a) AD 151, lost almost as new and disfigured by fire to which it gave an approximate date. (b) AD 140–4, showing the same design, Salus feeding serpent on altar.

recalled by central government just like ours. When lost by individuals it was hunted until found. Large coins like the *sestertii* were found again more easily than the small inflation bronzes of later years. If there are coins beneath your feet, they are more likely to be these latter and in fairly poor condition. The man who lost a *sestertius* or a *denarius* had more pressing reason than even today's most addicted collector to find them.

Roman coins have come down directly to those of us living within the confines of the old Empire. Our homes and gardens are on soil tamed by their civilisation. American, Japanese and Australian collectors are only too enviously aware of that. However, it is worth bearing in mind that Rome extended a presence well beyond the frontiers. While the 'Roman coin' which a Portuguese scholar recorded as being found in the West Indies in the sixteenth century can be dismissed as either a stray or a touch of diarist's colour, other finds cannot be so easily passed over.

Roman coins have been found in Ireland, Finland and across Russia. East Africa, southern India and Pakistan have produced considerable hoards. Roman gold has even been found in the Mekong Delta. In the final years of the Republic, Roman legionaries settled in a *colonia* on Chinese territory. Roman emissaries were recorded by China's ruling Han dynasty in the second century AD, sent by one *An-Tun*, better known to us as Marcus Aurelius (*Antoninus*). Earlier, in Domitian's day, the Chinese military ruler of Central Asia had sent an abortive mission to make contact with the Romans in Syria. Either bewildered or worn out, their ambassador turned back at the Persian Gulf.

As a collector's rule of thumb for these tough survivors, the most likely metals to be found on dealers' trays will be bronze, copper, orichalcum and silver – in that order. Chronologically these will tend to be Republican *denarii*, first and second century Imperial *asses* and *dupondii*, second century *sestertii*, base *antoniniani* from the third century and, lastly those all-pervading later small bronzes. Just as tough as their larger brothers, they deserve as much respect. They can also form a fascinating and economical collection, far richer and more diverse than the stolid, machined farthings and halfpennies which are their modern counterparts (Fig. 45). In one part of eighteenth-century England, small Roman bronze coins from the local fields actually passed into circulation as farthings. The episode says almost as much about the condition of the coins as it does about their finders' sense of thrift.

45. *Ae 2 and 3* of the fourth century, their reverses reflecting military pre-occupations of the time. (a) and (b) Delmatius, AD 335–7, **Rome mint, Glory of the Army** series. (c) Constans, AD 337–50, *centenionalis*, **ANT(ioch) mint**; Emperor dragging barbarian from hut – with the incongruous legend **The Good Times are Back !** (d) Constantius II, AD 337–61, *centenionalis*, Section **3 SIS(cia)mint**; Vetranius, Constantius' ally against Magnentius, holds standards. (e) Magnentius, usurper AD 350–3, *centenionalis*, **AMB(ianum) mint**; Magnentius spears an enemy. (These are in EF condition: in lesser grades they are quite common and can be bought for £1 or less, depending on the reign, type, mint and condition.)

III

HOW TO FIND THEM

When Vespasian's son Titus objected to his imposing a
tax even on the urinals, he passed a coin (*pecuniam*) from
the first takings under his nostrils, asking whether he was
upset by any smell. When Titus shook his head, Vespasian
snorted, 'Strange! It's fresh out of the urine!'
Suetonius, *Vespasian 23*, c. AD 115

The market and where to start

If so many Roman coins have survived – like the word *vespasiano*, still
the local slang in Rome for a public urinal – where are they all now?
Many are in museums and more are in collections. Museums sometimes sell off their surplus (see Fig. 118b) and even exchange their stock
to fill gaps, as would any collector. Collections are being broken up all
the time to realise cash, either for the original owner or for his heirs.
The vast bulk of coin is in continual commercial circulation, constantly
drip-fed by new finds.

It might be as well for the hunter to start by simply looking in a
museum, a haven away from price-tags and profits. On a showcase
with a comprehensive range of Roman coins, particularly in towns
which were once Roman settlements, the eye can be trained quite
quickly in the colour and condition of the real thing. Often, of course,
they will be in better condition than the collector will be able to afford
to buy in a shop; just as often they will be samples from a 'dig', in
worse condition than any collector might want to own yet still priceless
for the story they tell to the archaeologist.

After a museum it would be worth taking up the address of a local
coin society (numismatic club, coin and medal collectors' association –
the names vary but the purpose is the same). These are to be found
in most towns and are a source of much goodwill towards the fellow-
collector, not to mention advice, contacts and numerous exchanges.

Finally, properly prepared and preferably accompanied, the collector might take the plunge and attend a coin fair. These are regularly
advertised in collectors' publications. He should look along the trays.
It is well worth rummaging in the boxes of loose coins sold at a fixed

price. Prices should be compared from table to table. In short, like any shopper, the collector has to 'shop around'. I walk the full circuit of a coin fair before buying anything, making mental note of what I would like and what I can afford. It is important to take both time and a magnifying glass.

One dealer might be handling mainly ancient while another may have a few Roman oddments on a table laid out with medieval and modern coins. There is no ready conclusion to be drawn from either combination, but there are possibilities. The dealer with only a few ancients may have had them some time, may not be interested in Roman and may be glad for a return of his cash plus a small profit if only to keep stock moving. Sometimes he may simply not know anything about them and be glad to let the buyer take a 'job lot' for the sake of his own cash flow. His main profits after all will not come from a few Roman strays. If he has labelled a *sestertius* of Postumus as 'Roman coin' then the collector has found a bargain and both will be happy with the purchase (see Fig. 63a). On the other hand he may ask an inflated price hoping that someone will be ready to pay over the top.

Another possibility is that the dealer specialising in ancients may have a lower price for common starter material. His profits come completely from his ancients, however, and he may be selling at fairs for high prices. Little is likely to get past his experienced scrutiny. A part-time dealer may be selling for pin money, in which case his profit margin may be low. On the other hand, he may depend very much on a weekend's takings and therefore charge high prices. Fortunately, a man cannot make a living out of one 'fast buck'. Once bitten, his customers will not return or follow up his address card. Other dealers, too, will soon shun him or shop him. They need to keep their good name. He needs a returning clientele. Coins have to be sold; high prices can mean slower turnover and without turnover there is no recoup of outlay or buying in of fresh stock. With this in mind the collector should not hesitate to bid against the marked price; offering 25 per cent less may prove to be an acceptable compromise.

The question of prices is complex. Because inflation is now part of the texture of economic life, today's prices tend to be outdated by tomorrow. It pays to chat to the dealers and listen to them talking to their neighbouring stallholders. In this way the collector can learn if there is a demand or if coins are hardly moving at all. A buyer's market is a place for bargains. A 'bargain price' seems to be somewhere in the middle of the following reference points:
(a) what the addicted collector is ready to pay for a piece;
(b) a general market norm for that coin – across a giant spectrum centred on current auction figures;
(c) condition, rarity, popularity of particular issues;
(d) the amount the dealer originally paid for it and the profit margin which would content him after any reduction.

The 'junk shop' is now hard to find, although it has been reborn and facelifted in the form of the 'antique shop', depending on its locale and degree of self-conscious sophistication. Some have become general 'collector shops' and are worth a visit by the Roman coin collector. The hunter armed with his knowledge can still find bargains. In very recent years I have picked up a Trajan first-issue *sestertius* (ancient Rome's equivalent of the First Day Cover in philately) and a countermarked *sestertius* of Claudius (see Figs 99 and 110), both very desirable coins, cheap and, in the case of one of them, from a button-and-brooch bowl.

The coin fair and the casual find in such a shop are still no substitute for building up relations with one or more dealers. A network of contacts for mutual benefit can be formed around the country. Friendships grow. I have done business with a teacher, a hairdresser and a policeman, all dealing part-time in Roman coins. Magazine advertisements indicate postal lists. List prices can be compared. Offers such as 'Now sent post free' or 'Last year's prices still unchanged – to clear' might be worth taking up. The postal dealer wants to keep his customers like any other; he also has few overheads. The fear of long-distance swindle is negligible since coins are always sent on approval. Experience quickly teaches that one man's standards are higher than another's or that his grading terms are more accurate than others'. Invariably, I have found courtesy and helpful contacts through the post and have taken some of my most interesting coins from these sources. At times they will append a note as to where the coin originated – 'Bottom of brick kiln' (see Fig. 39), 'Roadworks in Chichester, 1974' (see Fig. 94) or simply 'Bought from navvy in Spain'. Some dealers have an additional list of Roman antiquities such as 'Arrowhead from Hadrian's Wall', 'Lamp from catacombs dated with label, 1894', 'Bronze dog, four inches long' and even 'Fourth century forgers' moulds, found near Cairo'. There is, of course, always the danger of being lured into setting up a domestic museum.

One antiquity of the Roman world of particular interest to the coin collector is the engraved jewel and even cameo stone. These are less expensive than might be imagined and, like some coins, they are often objects of great if battered and chipped beauty. Scholars have discovered direct links between some intaglio-cut gemstones and certain coin dies, (see p. 98). In the case of the cameo stone, certain examples can definitely be said to be by master artists as opposed to apprentices or even moonlighting mint-workers (Fig. 46).

Certain advertisements are to be avoided carefully: the glossy magazine advertisement in colour offering 'Silver Nero *tetradrachma* of Egypt' ('billon' in much smaller letters) for 'only £30'. The offer looks attractive until the collector finds the same coins on dealers' trays for anything between £6 and £18 each. Spotting the lure before the trap is part of the enjoyment of the hobby.

Postal dealing, however satisfactory, is still conducted over an inconvenient distance. Today, because of the growth of the hobby 'industry',

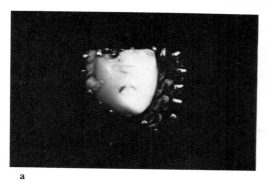

a

b

46. (a) Broken cameo (white and dark blue banded stone) of Gorgon Medusa, *c.*
AD 150, reset as modern ring. Even the photographer feared the reflective glare
from this traditional charm against the 'evil eye', still the bane of popular
Mediterranean culture. Originally an oval (2.3 × 3 cm), probably a pendant.
(b) First century *sestertii* showing Nero and Domitian wearing the head of
Medusa as a pendant charm, known as an *aegis*. Minerva also carries the image
on her shield, hence its portrayal from the back (see Fig. 142).

there is a coin centre of some kind in or near most people's home town.
The collector should go regularly and watch the trays and prices. The
proprietor often has a fund of good advice to offer (when the shop is
quiet). He may operate a deposit and lay-away scheme for painless
buying. Much of the trade gossip about the state of the market will
come his way. His customer, after all, is not a competitor and he is
building up a mutually beneficial relationship of trust. He may have
rummage-boxes under the counter containing unidentified or unpriced
Roman oddments. He may not be a Roman specialist and if coins look
unattractive a dealer may be happy to let them go for a small return
and even in bulk at a reduced price.

From such boxes come the worn samples to test out an electrolyte
cleaner (see Cleaning bronze and copper by electrolysis on p. 180). An
apparently 'damaged' coin may turn out to be countermarked under
the accumulated surface grime (Fig. 47a). There may be a Jewish
'grape-pip' labelled 'Carthaginian copper' by mistake – the palm tree

47. (a) *As* of Augustus, 7 BC, Lurius Agrippa moneyer; flatstruck as well as worn and countermarked **A(V)** behind the bust in a later reign when its value was questionable (£2, 1979). (b) *Lepton*, Coponius, Prefect of Judea and Samaria AD 6–9, (see Ch. VII) (£1, 1978).

design on the small coppers is remarkably similar (Fig. 47b). There is little to lose from buying a damaged or worn rarity which would otherwise be beyond the collector's purse. More often than not the coins most frequently encountered will be worn (but interesting) provincial bronzes and the all-pervading small change of the house of Constantine onwards.

Sometimes the dealer may pick up a cheap 'clutch' from a farmer or a traveller's handful from abroad. Obviously he will take out what he feels is worth marketing; what is left can be an attractive proposition at bulk price to both beginner and to the advanced collector. Unwanted items sometimes sell elsewhere and in turn can help to finance a growing collection.

By way of illustration, the finds of a field walker over a few months came to a local dealer. From the encrusted green pile he took what he felt would sell after a touch with the brush. The remaining ninety-seven coins I bought for £8.50 (Fig. 48). They ranged from a worn but distinct *sestertius* of Domitian (see Fig. 49b), through the second century coppers and third century debased silver to a large group of later small bronzes. Some of the earlier large bronze coins were worn almost beyond interpretation. Evidently they enjoyed a long circulation before loss, well into the years of third-century inflation. Others proved more interesting after cleaning – an unusual *semis* of Nero, a plated *antoninianus* of Gallienus, broken to determine its quality (see Fig. 36) and several deliberately fractured fourth-century bronzes made into even smaller small change (see Figs 53 and 147).

Along these various avenues the collector also learns much about numismatics in general, through the constant fingertip scrutiny of the rummager. Tiny battered Spanish pieces with the scroll wrapped round a pillar hint at the origin of the strange symbol for the US dollar. The faces from television epics set in Tudor times start to reappear in profile on hammered English silver. I have already mentioned the bell-metal coins of the French Revolution and the small Tsarist silver with the pathos it evokes of emigrés and a bygone age.

48. A field-walker's clutch: surface finds over several months (see Figs 49b and 53). The number of featureless discs support the theory that worn first- and second-century coins formed more than a third of those in circulation *c.* AD 250 (£8.50, 1980).

Thumbing through Germany's inflation notes of the 1920s is a sobering experience for those of us who feel we have suffered from present-day inroads into our values. These notes range from thousands of Reichsmarks through to not merely millions but milliards. There are even concentration-camp notes to be found, the commonest being those of Westerbork in Holland, printed in deceitful factory canteen style to greet the final mass arrest of Dutch Jews in 1944. Anne Frank was taken there that summer; the SS Commandant signatory of the notes she may have handled was leading a respectable existence in Düsseldorf as late as 1964. The list of numismatic sideroads is endless, informative and at times quite moving.

By this time the collector should be beginning to feel at home in the world of the Roman coin market. He may send for the auction catalogues of the famous London firms – Christie's, Vecchi/Schwer,

Spink, Sotheby – even if only to window-gaze. The notes and fine photographs are often highly informative and even on a limited budget some of the job lots might be tempting: 'Roman bronze lot (100), mostly fourth century and poor – estimated price £100' or 'Judea bronze lot (93) including *lepta* and city coins, fair to fine – estimated price £50'. However, it should be noted that these catalogues are far from cheap and only a small proportion of the annual output contain ancients.

Perhaps the biggest step for many will be a trip to London to view lots on offer at such auctions. The private budget collector should feel as welcome at the great auction houses as the dealer and the investor with his petrodollars. Obviously the latter will have greater buying power but the illustrated choice coins (see, for example, Fig. 37) do not make up the bulk of an auction. Nor is the 'estimated price' necessarily the buying price which may in some cases be much lower, particularly in the case of the more specialist ancients such as the Judea lot mentioned previously. It cannot be stressed too often that lots should be viewed before purchase. The dross often found in a job lot can outweigh the small number of coins in the lot which are worth buying. Even illustrated lots can be flattered by the camera when a 500 W floodlight hints at a lustre which may not even exist.

Frequently the more advanced collector may see a coin which he knows from experience can be found at coin fair or on postal list much less expensively tagged. It is not a delusion. Nor in such a case is the price 'topped up' to pay for a name or for overheads. Just as with any reputable dealer, the expertise and guarantee is included in such a price. In addition to this there is the convenience of avoiding a search of years, the immediacy of acquisition and the instant service in seeking out wanted coins – all of which in turn do generate some additional overhead costs. How much petrol, not to mention time and money wasted on low grade substitutes is spent in hunting for a certain coin? The collector conveniently forgets this! To stumble on a good *sestertius* at an equally 'good' price is a matter of sheer luck.

The collector on a budget will probably baulk at the initial outlay on a job lot, even though the actual cost of each coin may turn out to be a fraction of that paid over a counter when bought individually. If his bank manager can see that unwanted coins from such a lot will be resold in turn to finance the collecting, then he may give the budget collector a warm and helpful welcome. A common, mistaken belief is that small dealers and coin fairs have only the leftovers from the large established firms and that they are on the whole cheaper. An equally common misconception is that the major firms serve exclusively the trade and the wealthy. Neither is true. Coins do climb the rungs of a price ladder but they all start on the bottom rung: some of those highly priced items in small dealers' trays should never have been allowed off that bottom rung.

Friends go away on holiday and want to bring back a memento. If it is within the old Roman Empire, a coin from the market place might be suggested. Many people have an unwanted Roman coin stuck away in some tin or drawer, but here the collector needs to be tactful lest he earn a reputation for having no other subject of conversation. Coins may be good company – but not on their own. This chapter began with the problem of how to find them. It might now pose an equally pertinent question – how do you *stop* finding them?

Condition and quality

The eye is the best gauge of quality in a coin. The various accepted codes of description are only a form of agreed shorthand for the look and the feel. Grading has been bluntly described as 'an art, not a science'. (Those who have been stung by incorrect and loaded grading might be forgiven for feeling that it is a confidence trick.) There are even different grading scales adopted in different countries and numismatic circles. Certainly, the use of 'fair' or 'fine' takes on a different meaning from its everyday usage and even from the technical use of the same word by another dealer. 'Buyer beware' is perhaps the best advice this section can give.

That said, there are points to look for which can guide the collector's judgement of quality, financial considerations apart. As the first rule of thumb, look for the high spots on the surface of the coin (Fig. 49). In the majority of cases they will be worn, save in the case of a coin protected from centuries of handling by a kind environment. Are the letters flattened or have they still an edge to them? Is the hair worn smooth? (This is perhaps the most fragile part of the stamped metal and the first to suffer since it is also a high point.) Is the hair flattened uniformly or is the part nearest the field still visibly engraved? Is the wreath flush with the head or is at least its outline and at best its individual laurel leaves still discernible? Are the ears worn flat round a tiny hole or is there still the definite shape of pinna and lobe? Occasionally a coin may be considered **worn** when in fact it has been lightly struck or produced with a very shallow die. A coin may have been **flatstruck** by a weaker and more misdirected blow than usual, the last production piece of the shift (Fig. 50, see also Fig. 88).

Just as much as in any other hobby or even walk of life there are prejudices, blind spots and conservative ideas about condition among both dealers and collectors. These are sometimes understandably based on fairly outdated scholarship. Old ideas stick and are handed down in popular publications unchecked and unchanged like the proverbial dog's bad name. In addition, as if dealing with modern silver, gold and proofs, some will underestimate and underprice coins which

a

b

c

d

e

f

g

h

49. Conditions of coin. A Roman coin is rarely classed above **Good EF** (Fig. 37 is exceptional). Coins with high relief retain a bold profile even in **Poor** while low relief coins tend to wear flat across. There is a tendency among dealers to overgrade rare or popular coins, stressing rarity rather than condition: e.g. the *sestertius* of Nero will tend to be more in demand than one of Hadrian or Antoninus Pius, more commonly found. Where a coin has two grades, e.g. **Fair–Fine**, it is described as overall between these two conditions; where it is represented as **Fair/Fine**, it means that the obverse is **Fair** while the reverse is **Fine**. (a) and (b) could be described as **Poor**, **Fair**, **Mediocre** or even **Good** (which is in fact a low grade). The features of (b) are more distinct than (a) while the latter is bolder and more attractive. The legend on both is just about discernible and there is corrosion on (b). The collector might have reasons for wanting Hadrian (a) rather than Domitian (b) but in this condition it is pointless to quibble about grades since both *sestertii* are, by any standards, 'bad'! (£1 each or less, 1981). (c) Would be described as **F(ine)**, where Domitian's head and the legend are quite clear in outline but not in detail. Much would now depend on the design of the reverse, in this case similar to Fig. 21b, hence the price of £12 in 1979. (d) Shows more detail about the wreath and face and the hair is more distinct; Nerva is not commonly encountered in *sestertius* form and this, together with a standard reverse (Fortuna) would place the coin at **G(ood) F(ine)**, hence the price of £30 in 1980. (e) While **N(early) V(ery) F(ine)** is of a relatively common Emperor and has some pitting damage. The sestertius is boldly struck and Antoninus Pius shows in much better detail than Nerva; the reverse shows the Temple of Roma in **V(ery) F(ine) plus** and yet, due to the unpredictability of markets, the coin cost only £13 in 1982. (f) Antoninus' beard, hair, laurel leaves and most of the legend are crisp in detail although signs of circulation wear are beginning to show; with a common reverse (Salus and serpent) this **V(ery) F(ine)** coin seemed overpriced at £50 in 1981. (g) The *sestertius* of Nero is certainly **V(ery) F(ine)** and a good one at that; in fact it is nearer **E(xtremely) F(ine)** save for the surface cracks, and slightly flatstruck lettering behind the bust; Nero's *sestertii* always command a high price – at £650 in 1981 this was no exception. (h) An **E(xtremely) F(ine)** double-*centenionalis* of Magnentius is about as perfect as can be expected for a coin of its age which has seen brief circulation, shown by the incipient signs of wear at the back of the head (£660, 1981).

50. *As*, Augustus, 7 BC. Flatstruck rather than just worn (see also Fig. 88).

have been pierced, plated or in any way broken (Fig. 51). What of a coin which has been worn to nothing but which carries a good crisp countermark. Is it 'poor' or 'fine'? There are many chinks in the market armour. Coins instanced in this section may not be of finest gallery bloom but they are often of good quality and packed with potential interest.

'Why do you want that?' asked a dealer as I took a copper disc from a rummage box (see Fig. 101b). Its shape suggested it had once been a coin. I paid him a few pence and pointed to the 6 mm countermark sunk into the blank. 'Depends what turns you on, doesn't it!' he grinned. True, it took a glass and some time to fathom the mark. It was the miniature bearded head of an Emperor with a three-letter legend, engraved with watchmaker's precision and preserved by being countersunk. In itself it is a die-stamp, a coin within a coin. The bevelled edge of the flan tells me it is eastern, perhaps of Commagene. The beard tells me it is after Hadrian. I have seen trays of fine, large provincial bronzes, unidentified and priced at a couple of pounds each. They are riddled with unknown countermarks on top of easily discernible legends and portraits. Lack of handbook and time, as well as the hurdle of the Greek language, has put many collectors and dealers off these potentially rewarding pieces.

The **pierced** coin is an interesting case. Sometimes it has weakened the metallic structure and encouraged corrosion or fracture. (There are even conditions of piercing!) When, however, it is remembered that the body itself was used as a bank, that wedding dowries and talismanic metals (moon silver, sun gold and orichalcum) were customary decorations, then the holing of a *denarius* or *drachma* can be seen as part of its use as a coin. Similarly with traces of **mounting, pendant loop marks** and **claw mount scratches**, all of which will reduce the price of a coin. I have a 'tribute penny' of Tiberius in otherwise attractive condition, but reduced to a mere £20 because of a spot of silver soldering on the reverse design (Fig. 52).

A once-mounted coin may be unusual or aesthetically pleasing – the elephant *denarius* of Titus, the moon *denarius* of Hadrian (see Fig. 128c). While body-wear will have taken it out of the normal damage from the circulation, there is still the friction-wear caused by chain, thread or the next coin, as on a row of military medals today. Sometimes a good guesstimate can be made of the length of time it swung from neck or ear. Sometimes the hole has been **plugged** and not always for aesthetic reasons. The original hook or rivet might still be there, as in Fig. 128c. More often it is a device meant to deceive and is commonly found in gold or rare silver. The *hemidrachma* in Fig. 115 might be such a case. It is worthwhile taking a glass and examining a coin for jewellery or plugging traces at around '12 o'clock', in the field and at intervals round the circumference if the coin has been claw-mounted.

Scholars are still in debate over the **plated** silver coin, particularly

51. Broken coins: (a) *denarius*, Hadrian, AD 117–38, corn and poppy in grain bin (found on the banks of the Thames, London). (b) *follis*, Licinius I, Section **3 AQ(uileia) mint**, AD 312, Roma in Temple. (£1 each, 1980).

52. *Denarius*, Tiberius, AD 14–37, Lyons mint. Popular as the 'tax coin' of the Gospels, reduced to £20, 1981, due to silver solder on reverse.

the first century *denarii* which are found in considerable number. Too little is known to dismiss them as forgeries. Sometimes the plating and the die is of high quality and may carry a banker's testmark which failed to break through to the base core beneath. Some coins described in good faith as silver may also be plated, the surface as yet uncracked. Plated coins frequently have as much artistic merit as the pure silver version (see pp. 109–12 and Fig. 106).

53. Fractionalised bronze, fourth century, Constans or Constantius II. A **FEL TEM** on the reverse puts it after *c*. AD 348. Two or three such 'coins' can be made from one small bronze, cut into almost circular shape by a narrow-bladed clipper. Britain was chronically short of currency at several stages during the Roman occupation (7 mm.).

A coin may be described as **broken** or **damaged** when it is really **fractionalised** or **halved**. When the early Empire was struggling to establish an international coinage or when the later Empire was trying to keep coinage going in the teeth of inflation, there were inevitable problems of supply. A coin might be deliberately halved or fragmented to provide several lower denominations (Fig. 53). I have seen on a dealer's tray a crocodile *as* of Nîmes (Nemausus) priced at about £20 while the halving of the same denomination was priced at over £30! On the other hand, a plated *denarius* of the late second century might be found broken for other reasons, much as the lead florins of George V are handed on bent, chopped into segments or showing a nailhole in the middle, literally 'nailed to the counter'.

Sometimes a coin is **repaired**. A silver *denarius* had a cracked flan from birth. In later years the crack has given under stress (Fig. 54).

54. *Denarius*, Augustus, 2 BC–AD 11, Lyons mint. Augustus' adopted grandsons in adult togas carry the silver spears and shields of manhood. Broken and repaired (£8, 1979).

A silversmith (or superglue) has joined the two pieces together, often with little sign to show beyond the hairline crack common to the flan of many Roman coins. As with plugging, repair can also be done with intent to deceive.

Damage can cover many other more serious inflictions. There is the gouge-mark, sometimes bringing the price of a valuable and otherwise good coin very low indeed (see Fig. 142a). There are the digs and scratches of whatever period, sometimes from a finder's trowel (Fig. 55). There are also deliberate defacements marking the change of ruler. At the end of 'Caligula''s reign and possibly after Allectus died in rebel Britain, the population wreaked its pent-up feelings on the nearest symbol of government to hand – the bust or mintmark of a coin (Fig. 56). In Italy and Germany today the hacked out *fasces* and swastikas on public buildings still draw attention to the fury of a population discovering it had been mislead. *Damnatio memoriae* as the Romans called it can form a cheap but evocative part of any collection. Roman monuments still show the chiselling away of names like Gaius 'Caligula' and Domitian. Nothing changes. One winter's night in Moscow, my family spent a frozen few moments near the Eternal Flame on the Soviet War Memorial. The plinth commemorating Stalingrad has been cleverly changed to the new name Volgograd by prising out the first of two marble panels. However well done, minute chisel marks on the joint still tell their tale.

Creased is a description found frequently on hammered Tudor or Stuart silver but rarely on Roman. When found in this condition such coins tend to be the thin base silver *antoniniani* of the later third century and the thinnest of silver from the end of the next century. The **clipped** coin is often found among the silver of the same period (see Fig. 43). Much more common is the coin with a damaged and a fine side. It might be described as 'Very Fine/Poor', obverse and reverse in that order. A good coin of 'Caligula' will set me back a considerable

55. *Sestertius*, Titus, AD 80, with common **Pax Augusti !** reverse. Scratched and worn on the high points it cost £9 in 1978 as opposed to several hundred for the VF version in 1982.

56. (a) *As*, Gaius 'Caligula', *c.* AD 37. The bust has been defaced with a star punch; Vesta is almost 'religiously' unscathed. The defacement is as worn as the coin, therefore contemporary with the coin's earliest years. One ancient source reports Gaius' bronze as being withdrawn in AD 44 to dishonour him and because a 'Gaian *as*' was a proverbially bad coin. A statue was made of the first batch to be returned (£9, 1974). (b) 'quinarius' Allectus. AD 293–6, possibly defaced at his death (£1, 1979).

sum, but one with an obliterated reverse and a good bold portrait can be had at a very low price indeed – even lower if the damage is the other way round, since most collectors go for portraits. To me such a coin is a bargain (Fig. 57). I have seen the purist shake his head and dismiss it as 'rubbish'.

Pitting is another form of damage inflicted upon a coin, sometimes by an instrument, sometimes simply by the ravages of time and soil. A glass will show whether the marks hide anything more than pitting, as for instance the legionary title in Fig. 12. **Wear** might also be due to bad alloying of the metal at the mint furnace. Some second and third century coins have streams and patches of copper running through their orichalcum alloy. The unmixed copper gives way to wear more quickly than the surrounding harder metal (Fig. 58).

Cleaning is undoubtedly a form of damage. A coin may have been polished like a horsebrass. It may have been acid-stripped of its pro-

57. *As*, Gaius 'Caligula', *c*. AD 37, which has evidently been face down in preservative clay or silt; the reverse is severely damaged. The collector would be attracted to the portrait alone for £30 in 1982 (a financial blow softened by part exchange!). Possibly shortage of coin under Claudius prevented the recall of Gaius' coin becoming effective. Were the reverse condition to match that of the obverse the coin would fetch at least £300 in 1982.

58. *Sestertii*, Marcus Aurelius. (a) AD 164, showing bands of dark, unmixed copper in front of and behind the bust (£1, 1979). (b) Contemporary *sestertius* in perfect condition (£900, 1981).

tective (and attractive) patina, leaving the coin looking brighter but as characterless and forlorn as a plucked chicken in a cold wind. **Patina** is the oxidization of the surface which has ceased and which in turn protects the metal beneath from further oxidization. It should be left.

'Plucking' a coin of its patina only lays open the underlying metal to more damage, like peeling skin from hand or foot; it also reveals 'goosepimples', the pitted undersurface formerly hidden by the patina. **Verdigris**, or 'bronze disease', a bright green powdery oxidization still in progress, is not desirable and can be removed (see Cleaning bronze and copper by electrolysis on p. 180). Careful examination needs to be made as the bright green spot could in fact already be patinated (Fig. 59). There are also many **dirty** coins, sometimes compacted in the crevices with grease and grime. They may be classed as 'fair' simply because the trouble has not been taken to clean the surface with softened water and a light brush.

Some coins patinate uniformly and this adds to their looks. **Toned** silver takes on the hue of gunsteel grey-blue (Fig. 60). As the orichalcum coins of the third century lose their zinc content for tin and lead, the patina takes on a mottled, multicoloured hue. A catalogue might enthuse as much about the patina as about the coin. One example (Superior, California, 1981) could even be describing a firework display. From plain green, brown and black, the spectacle flares into 'greenish brown', 'gorgeous reddish green', 'dark chocolate brown' and even 'desirable apple green'. While the faker can concoct instant patina of almost any kind, patination is still regarded by collectors as a good sign of authenticity. A caution is necessary: there may be some signs of working more detail than actually survives (and even new detail

59. *Sestertii*, Hadrian, *c.* AD 136 (see Fig. 128b). (a) Spots of oxidisation on the bust have patinated; Hadrian's beard was grown to hide facial blemishes, setting a fashion for a century afterwards (£4, 1980). (b) Contemporary *sestertius* in excellent condition (£100, 1982).

60. Toned silver of Vespasian. (a) *denarius*, AD 74, caduceus of health, toned to blue-grey (£5, 1980). (b) *hemidrachma* of Caesarea, Cappadocia, struck to help pay off troops after the Jewish war; toned black (£7, 1979).

altogether!) into the crystalline surface of the patina itself. It is known in the trade as **tooling**.

To understand and judge the quality of the Roman coin it is essential to know something of the workings of the mint. The collector may then be able to distinguish real damage and wear from lack of quality control, debasement and metal conservation by harassed administrations. He needs to look for the remains of countermarks, and the reasons for a coin being apparently badly struck. Worn dies, particularly the reverse, can produce apparently worn coins even when new (Fig. 61a). Undersized flans where the wording has slipped off the edge (Fig. 61b) and pancake flans where the metal puffs up at the edge like a piecrust can distract by their crudity until it is realised that these were the accepted standards of the day. A collector looking for the not-quite-round of the typical Roman coin should be prepared for virtually square *sestertii* from the second century and jagged, small *sestertii* fragments from the third – strip-struck, sheared and economising on metal in hard times (Fig. 62).

Prices are frequently based on looks. As by the chrome on the second-hand car, the buyer is drawn by a pleasing coin. The collector needs to learn that there is value and interest beyond the obvious and the more expensive. He needs to take advantage of this while it lasts. Markets change and the collector and dealer alike grow ever more sophisticated and aware.

61. (a) *Sestertii*, Severus Alexander, AD 222–35 and Gordian III, AD 238–44. Both have been double-struck, possibly with worn dies and wedge-cut to denote that they were substandard. Such cuts can easily be confused with flan-cracks, but on some coins the mark of the cutting tool is quite plain. (b) double *sestertius*, Postumus, AD 259–68, probably an overstrike onto an undersize flan (£110, 1981).

62. *Sestertii*, third century, struck on flans sheared from strips. (a) Pupienus (£80, 1982). (b) Philip (£60, 1982). (c) Volusian (£480, 1982). (d) Trajan Decius (£2, 1980).

IV

THE ARMCHAIR ARCHAEOLOGIST

> (Marcus Aurelius) promised the soldiers a bounty . . .
> 20,000 *sestertii* each for the other ranks, the rest propor-
> tionately more . . . (Elagabalus) never dined for less than
> 100,000 *sestertii*, that is, thirty pounds of silver. In fact,
> sometimes he dined at a cost of three million sesterces.
>
> **Anon.** *History of the Augusti*
> **fourth century** AD

Coins do not make sense on their own. To understand and make the most of collecting Roman coins it is essential that the collector spends a little money (and considerable time) on books. A small home library for the armchair archaeologist (for this is what the numismatist really is) could be divided into two shelves – the original writings of the Romans in translation supplemented by the basic modern studies of their coins. The reference libraries of our universities and museums are filled with somewhat forbidding works, usually out of the financial reach of the collector and just as frequently out of print after a limited edition for the specialist market has been exhausted. General libraries, on the other hand, carry little more than general collecting books with no more than a passing chapter on Roman coins and illustrated with the usual near-perfect specimens.

Books

Penguin Classics include a magnificent range of Roman writers, once inaccessible to all but the Latinist. Each one is replete with helpful notes and index, invaluable for quarrying coin references and personal details. Suetonius' *Twelve Caesars* is even illustrated with twelve coins and numismatic notes. A court historian of the early second century with an ear ever open for the gossip handed down in high places, Suetonius furnishes highly readable if scandalous detail of the lives 'at the top' and physical descriptions of his subjects of particular interest to the coin collector. He deserves careful reading. Even the worst of the tyrants had his better side: Nero, for instance, created an ombudsman to deal with complaints from slaves suffering maltreatment; Otho, for all his lechery and posing, died a brave death and was mourned. To the work of Suetonius might be added the *Lives of the Later Caesars* (*Historia Augusta*) by an unknown ancient author. Backed by modern critical notes, it acts as a sequel to Suetonius and rounds out our knowledge of the Roman princes up to ·the end of the reign of Elagabalus in AD 222. Incidentally, it contains the only known ancient record of the building of Hadrian's Wall.

Several other ancients deserve a place on this first shelf. Penguin Classics also publish the works of Tacitus, including his short pamphlets on Britain and Germany, his *Annals of Imperial Rome* covering the period AD 14–68 and his *Histories* covering the Flavian period (AD 69–96). The books are not complete but Tacitus, a contemporary of Suetonius, draws his picture with great strokes and much invented speech. At times he writes more like a playwright than a chronicler.

Josephus (Flavius), the Jewish rebel commander in Galilee who passed over to the Roman side during the Jewish War, wrote a history of the campaign published by Penguin as *The Jewish War*. Unfortunately his other major work, *The Antiquities of the Jews*, is not published alongside the more popular work on the rebellion. It can be found in the more expensive Loeb edition, divided into several volumes with Greek and English texts on facing pages. In the same series, of particular use to the serious coin collector, can be found Pliny Senior's *Natural History Book 33* on metals and minerals.

One further book which might be tagged onto the end of the shelf is the patchwork quilt of fact, legend and hagiography which is Eusebius' *Church History*, the attempt of a fourth-century bishop and friend of Constantine to bring together some of the fragmented records and oral traditions of early organised Christianity. He was in a good position to research his work since he was born and bred in Palestine itself and Bishop of Caesarea, the coastal administrative capital. The book is a useful,· interesting and, at times, revealing starting point for the story of the rise of the churches in the Roman Empire.

The second shelf of books should be the collector handbooks, ready for instant dipping (and even total immersion). With these to hand and a growing fingertip knowledge, the need for the specialist tome becomes less. They are, after all, an aid to, not a substitute for observation which is the only way to build up a body of knowledge not encompassed in any one book, however well written. The patient collector will find that he never stops learning.

Seaby publish *Roman Coins and Their Values* (1981) by David Sear. It contains a comprehensive set of introductory notes and myriad illustrations which make it the standard English handbook for collector and dealer alike. With good reason the 1981 edition is the fourth since 1964, each successive edition being revised up to date. (The date of a book's publication is important: it may be based on dated scholarship; it may be a convenient and decorative *reprint* of a famous but less than read-able nineteenth-century volume.) The values given in Sear's handbook are only an indication and are so dependent on factors such as con-dition, demand and the amount of material on a fluctuating market (see Ch. III) at any one time that they should be treated with 'inter-ested reserve' rather than regarded as definitive. At one inch thickness the book makes no pretence to be exhaustive in its coverage, unlike its companion volumes on *Roman Silver Coins and Their Values* now in the process of being revised and extended.

From the same stable, compiled by Peter Seaby and Frank Purvey, comes the more general *Coins of England and the United Kingdom* (1980) where the Roman interest is (understandably) confined to the opening sections and a simple representative catalogue of the main coins of Celtic and Roman Britain.

Gilbert Askew's *Roman Coinage of Britain* (1946) is now reprinted by Seaby and provides an unparalleled wealth of detailed background, however slightly dated. It is a good brief catalogue of all coins likely to be encountered by the collector in the British isles.

Sear's latest contribution to popular numismatics is *Greek Imperial Coins and Their Values* (1982) a guide to the 'local coinages' of the Roman Empire, replete with maps and nearly two thousand photographs. While it makes a valuable and fascinating handbook, it is expensive and the foregoing reservations about market values apply equally to this as to any such catalogue. The book approaches the whole subject chronologically, Emperor by Emperor, ranging across the localities for each reign. It could be argued that a geographical coverage, province by province, would be more convenient for the collector puzzled by a Greek local coin.

In 'coffee-table' format but backed by a formidable arsenal of schol-arship comes the simply titled *Roman Coins* (1978) by Dr J. Kent of the British Museum. In fine photographic detail, matching the quality of the absorbing text, some of the finest coins in the world are assembled under one cover to teach and to entertain both scholar and collector.

Stanley Gibbons Publications Ltd have published booklets on all periods of coin collecting. *Coins of Roman Britain* (1976) by David Millar, when obtainable is certain value for a very small outlay. Even better value for its price is Peter Casey's *Roman Coinage in Britain* (1980), published in the deservedly popular Shire Archaeology series, available from museums as well as from high-street bookshops. It discusses in scholarly but readable depth the metal content, the figures for hoards and for losses and is profusely illustrated. It is a commendable step in making sound numismatic scholarship available to Everyman. One final booklet, deceptively simply written and well-illustrated is *Coins and the Bible* (1975) by Martin Price, inexpensively published by Vecchi, the coin dealers of London.

A complete set of Roman coin texts would include *Coins of the Roman*

Empire in the British Museum (known as *BMC*, Mattingly and others commenced 1923) covering the period up to Balbinus and Pupienus, and the more complete series, *Roman Imperial Coins* (known as *RIC*, the latest volume appearing in 1981) covering the whole Roman period in immense detail to Athanasius. They are prohibitively expensive and require a small wheelbarrow for transportation. However, they are internationally recognised as the most comprehensive research on the subject in the English language. The collector who manages to purchase even one volume of the above two series, either in a second-hand shop or in a sale, should count himself fortunate.

I hope the reader is not insulted if I suggest how to use a book. Not all books are meant to be read from end to end – the Bible is a classic example. The index should be regarded as a tool for opening the book. If a particular heading cannot be found it may occur under an alternative subject. For example, 'coins' may not appear at all; it may be spread over the various denominations as well as under 'money', 'mint' and 'forgery'. Presuming the book is personal property, pencil notes in the margin can be useful reminders during future browsing. The book itself can be used as a storehouse for cuttings and additions to the book's own notes. It is also worth remembering that a page may be read ten times and only on the eleventh occasion does a certain sentence come to the reader's notice due to some recent 'experience' of a coin. I have a Postumus *sestertius*, one of the Roman Empire's last such, even if it is from a pretender (Fig. 63a). It has a neat rounded flan, too big for the die and too good for the third century. On reading Casey for the *n*th time, his passing remark that Postumus used many old *sestertii* for restriking suddenly made sense of the coin. A glass then revealed the faint remains of the earlier coin around the edge and the whole process was confirmed by the eccentric arcs of two different circumferences. Months later a double-*sestertius* of Postumus also came my way (Fig. 63b). An additional clue, the bright brassy orichalcum with a high proportion of zinc, pointed to the same background.

As the collector travels he will pick up other booklets from museums and from Roman sites. Postcards of coins, especially those from the British Museum, help to build up a mental picture in preparation for the moment when a coin comes the buyer's way at a good price. Catalogues from major auction houses are sometimes handbooks in themselves. Pricelists mailed regularly from dealers and often illustrated are also a useful part of the collector's archive.

Coin Monthly is a leading magazine in Britain for collectors, with a circulation which has varied between 14,000 and 19,000 per month. It carries a regular Ancients feature as well as a 'Question Box' to which rubbings and photographs may be sent for comment and occasionally publication. A courteous and illuminating reply is the end result. The magazine also lists coin fairs across England and contains a long series of classified advertisements from home and abroad. The

63. (a) *Sestertius*, Postumus, *c.* AD 265, *Colonia Agrippina* (Cologne), Gaul being raised by Postumus as '**Restitutor Galliae**' – **SC** has by this time disappeared. Traces of another legend show beyond the die edge behind the bust; the coin is too round, too fine in orichalcum and the eccentric die circumferences confirm it to be an overstrike on an earlier worn *sestertius* (£1, 1980). (b) double-*sestertius*, Postumus, with similar indications; tong-snips reflect bad handling of a reheated flan (see Fig. 61b and Fig. 94) (£12, 1981).

Roman collector will find himself keeping back numbers for reference. Another monthly published in both Britain and America is *Coin and Medal News* (formerly *Coin News* but now incorporating the Stanley Gibbons monthly *Coins and Medals*). It carries a range of articles across the whole numismatic spectrum, including an article on some aspect of ancient coins each month. After a number of years the specialist collector in ancient coins may find that he 'grows out of' the monthly general magazine as the articles inevitably come to contain little that is new to add to his amassed experience.

It is advisable to take a sample of any periodical before squandering a year's subscription which may be regretted. Seaby's *Coin and Medal Bulletin* and *Spink's Numismatic Circular* distil information about recent finds, sales and items of scholarly interest across the whole range of numismatics. From across the Atlantic come *World Coin News*, *The Numismatist*, *Numismatic International*, *Hoards* and even *Coinquest*, a magazine devoted entirely to the countermarks within coins!

Equipment

A magnifying glass is essential – I confess to having four! Most collectors have at least a large desk-glass and a small folding glass for the pocket. A standing illuminated magnifier or microscope – to my mind the height of collector luxury – allows the hands to be free for holding and pivoting a coin.

Once bought, coins have to be stored. It is advisable to keep them apart rather than have them jingling together in bag or box. For the man of some means there are tailormade cabinets with sliding drawers, locking doors and brass fittings – a stylish furniture finish to the hardwood necessary for their construction. Homemade items can be hazardous since the wrong wood will set up a chemical reaction in a whole collection. Old cabinets, sometimes needing only a good polish to make them presentable, can often be bought as end lots at major auctions. However beautiful the purpose-built cabinet may be, it does make a burglar's life a fraction easier than it should be.

As a temporary measure, most collectors follow the dealers by storing their coins in an indexed box containing plastic envelopes, each marked with a descriptive label, cost and the date of purchase. There has been some controversy over the PVC used in earlier and cheaper productions of these envelopes. 'Virgin' PVC is not totally inert and it is claimed that it causes slight damage, particularly to bronze coinage stored this way over a long term.

The final move for most collectors will be from box to album. There are tailormade albums to suit most sizes of coin and pocket. However, I must confess that I have never taken to them. Notes on the coins cannot be stuck over the plastic pocket, nor do they look sightly after the uneven surfaces of large Roman coins have made their indentations on other leaves in the album. Cardboard inserts between each page can help solve this problem and some albums do have rigid inserts already in place in the pockets of the plastic page. This still does not solve the problem of the flat-stuck flan, the *piedfort* or the very high-relief bust.

I offer a suggestion. My coins are probably more handled than are most private collections since they are also used for teaching. They need both protection and built-in information. Albums, however good, are not tailormade to the irregular size of the Roman coin unless card mounts are handcut for each individual striking. I buy one stationer's A4 ringbinder, preferably with four rings rather than two. To this I add as many transparent A4 pockets as are required. Using A4 quality cartridge paper I then design the layout of a page, cutting with a razorblade the shape of each coin and typing up any necessary notes. A hand-coloured title and date catches the eye and perhaps the interest. I then insert page into pocket and using four staples per coin fix the coins into each cut-out shape in the cartridge paper – starting from

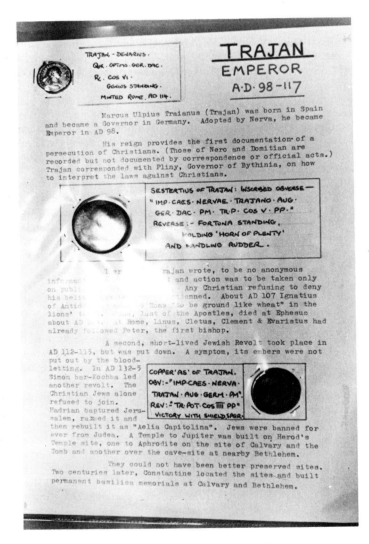

64. Sample page of notes and coins inserted into PVC folder.

the bottom, of course! The stapling of the plastic around the coin anchors it firmly within a pocket (Fig. 64). A page complete with coins and notes can then be taken out, used and reinserted with the minimum of trouble. The coin is protected from chip-greased and acidic fingers. The reading matter mounts up until such an album becomes a book in itself with real coins serving as the illustrations. Stiff cardboard cut to A4 size acts as a protective buffer between each sheet (or even as a stiffener within each folder). These inserts can be made both attractive and informative when covered with photographs of similar coins in better condition taken from booklets or catalogues. A note of caution: the number and condition of coins increases and improves as do the ideas and information about them. Keeping any album or exhibition up to date is time-consuming. It is also what the hobby is about.

My collection has 'appeared' several times on local radio. Without benefit of camera the interviewer (including one DJ on a morning chat-show) has to describe what he sees ('That big one – that coloured one'). Microphone leads enmesh us both as we pass coins to and fro over the sound equipment in intervals between the latest hit singles. One interviewer in fact did most of the interview blind to any coins at all because of his sound table. On another occasion, to bring them closer to listeners, we introduced sound effects by dropping coins into a glass ashtray or onto a small stone. It was difficult to suppress the mirth over a live microphone. We later discussed the possibility of an erudite series of programmes on coins which would need only a simple pile of assorted washers.

Cleaning

The general principle of coin-cleaning is 'Don't!' However, to know about cleaning is to be able to recognise it. The collector will find much well-meaning, often conflicting advice about cleaning. It generally causes damage and is regarded as such. It also takes away the character of a coin which has taken on the colour of many centuries and makes it lifeless.

In practice the collector can do a limited amount of cleaning without damage to the coin. Soap and/or simple softened water will remove any greasy film, recognisable as tacky to the touch. A soft brush either dry or with softened water can often work wonders with silver and bronze, but some say that bronze should not come into contact with water at all. Occasionally stubborn dry soil clings compacted in the crevices of a coin: a soft *wooden* toothpick may remove this with pleasing results as long as there is no corrosion damage beneath. Metal should never be used upon a coin as modern steels are inevitably stronger than soft and aged bronze or silver.

Silver tarnishes and there may be a temptation to use silver polish. This will brighten the coin but at the same time will take away a microscopic layer of the metal, thereby exposing it to further oxidization. The 'toned' coin should be left (see Fig. 60). Some collectors suggest a touch of thin oil or even a more permanent layer of thin transparent lacquer to give the coin a 'museum finish' and preserve it from further exposure to oxidization in the air. However, on the most uniformly patinated coin there can be spots where the process is still at work and the verdigris so sealed in reacts like rust sealed in under car paint – it breaks out in a very short period and makes the last state of the coin worse than the first. I have used beeswax on a totally verdigris-clear coin with most pleasing results, enhancing the patina and helping to preserve the condition of the coin. It goes without saying that there should be no abrasive action whatever on a coin, either with cloth (which is harsher than the fingers might suggest) or with metal polish (which is in fact an acidic abrasive).

Small electrolytic cleaners are marketed where the coin is attached to one terminal of a tranformer, then immersed into a pint of water, salt and a touch of citric acid. My youngest son gleefully describes this as 'cooking coins'. It does remove verdigris. It can make more sense of a badly corroded coin, although it will hardly increase its value. The current in solution changes the oxidization back into a metal film. The instructions should be adhered to with great care and better coins left alone.

The so-called Bath Hoard (Fig. 65) was in part treated by electrolysis but without the salt and acid. Instead, water-softener was added to the water and the finished coins coated with beeswax. The results are to my mind magnificent, the closest I have yet seen to real coin-cleaning while leaving both patina and metal totally unaffected (see Cleaning bronze and copper by electrolysis on p. 180). Perhaps the purist could still object (Fig. 66).

The subject of cleaning is as rife with horror-stories as it is with advice. Collectors have been known to use brake-fluid, paintstripper and hydrochloric acid. In my early enthusiasm I used solutions which I cannot bring myself to describe – fragile coins literally disappeared into bubbles in the solution. More harm than good comes from drastic impatient attempts to do the impossible. The strongest solution will still not 'clean' corrosion since corrosion is a change in the metal itself. Where this change has taken place evenly and preserved the original form of the metal – crystalline patina – it has ceased and has now become a protective. No collector in his right mind would want to strip it to get at some non-existent 'better coin' hidden underneath. Even where visible soil is removed on a recently unearthed bronze coin, damage is often made only more obvious and the regretful conclusion will be that they were better left soiled. At least they gave a more wholesome impression when their defects were packed out with foreign matter.

65. Close-up of part of the Bath Hoard after cleaning (see Fig. 40)

66. *As*, Domitian, AD 86, **Moneta Augusti** issue. (a) Prior to cleaning by the method described on p. 180. (b) After cleaning (£2, 1979).

Themes

There are good reasons for concentrating a collection into themes. They provide a sense of direction, paths in an otherwise vast terrain. Otherwise the collector might stumble in every direction, simply amassing without making such headway. A theme, as it grows, provides a great sense of satisfaction.

There are two extremes in approaching a thematic collection. One is to start by obtaining whatever is available, place it in a box and shake it to suggest a theme – even if it is specialising mainly in worn unrecognisable bronzes. The other extreme is to collect all the known variations of, for example, Otho's silver coinage. This latter is quite rare, alleviated by no bronze save from a few provinces. The theme would be exhausted almost as quickly as would the collector's bank account.

Between the extremes lie a hundred different avenues. I began, as many do, by trying to obtain the portraits of the first twelve Caesars, a difficult task when it comes to Otho and still not easy when trying to find Gaius 'Caligula' who for obvious reasons of notoriety is much in demand and whose bronze coins seem to have been recalled in part after his *damnatio memoriae*. Suetonius' *Lives* provides useful facial details of each of the twelve Emperors in this theme. At the same time, since this was also the century of the rise of Christianity, I became interested in New Testament coinage, particularly after finding a couple of Judean bronzes in a souvenir handful from the Jerusalem marketplace.

The collector of portraits will quickly learn that just as hairstyles change from decade to decade (Fig. 67), so too portraits change, even within a single reign. There are more reasons for this than a simple change of shift among the die-sinkers. Domitian's face changes so much between AD 77 and 85 that a new collector might be forgiven for thinking they were two different people. Trajan is one person on his first issue coins and another on his last issues (see Figs 109 and 110). Nero's faces may lack variety – amply compensated by his many hairstyles – but they make a gallery of jowls and chins with its own distinct fascination. In lower grades of condition the smaller Neronian coppers are quite plentiful and cheap. AD 64 produced its own particular European coin 'mountain' which stayed in use for a good two centuries and is still being tapped by collectors today.

While on a patient long-term search for theme coins within my financial reach, I came across attractive coins of the later Roman Emperors. Another theme and another album devoted to later coinage and mint-curiosities began to develop. The original first-century album now had its completed twelve portraits, although a battered Alexandrian *tetradrachmon* had to serve for Otho – it shows his toupé quite clearly (see Fig. 108). An appendix was added to take the occasional coins of relatives of the twelve Caesars.

67. Ladies' hairstyles: (a) *Sestertius*, Agrippina, *c.* AD 37. (b) *dupondius*, Antonia, AD 41. (c) Faustina Senior, posthumous and veiled, after AD 141. (d) Faustina Junior, *c.* AD 165. (e) Julia Domna, *c.* AD 200.

The later stylised portraits of the time of the Tetrarchs onwards could form another theme for the collector interesting himself in the development of art. Whose nose appears in the fractionalised coin of Fig. 53? A collection might be built up of the house of Constantine or even as many portraits and mints as possible of the Emperor Constantine himself, one of Rome's few rulers to be proclaimed from the wastelands of Yorkshire. The variations of helmet alone worn by this one ruler could provide material for another theme! (Fig. 68).

Themes beget themes just as A roads lead to B roads. The twelve Caesars did not see out the first century and Nerva's coins are quite striking pieces of portraiture while Trajan's coins are easily obtained. 'Sets' can become attractive even without the prohibitively costly gold. At least two of the *tres monetae* (as the Romans themselves called the set of three money metals) could be shown from the *denarius* down to the common coppers. In the case of Jewish coins (which carry no portraits), once I had all the Prefects and Procurators of Judea represented in tiny *lepta* or 'grape-pips' as the Jews may have called them, it seemed natural to turn to the variety of other coins which feature in the Gospels (see Ch. VII).

The history of the denominations could be shown. A *sestertius* from each emperor or at least from each decade would make a splendid display showing the rise and fall of Rome's most artistic coin from its beginnings under Augustus to its final demise under Postumus when

68. Helmets: (a) Constantine in parade helmets on *Ae 3*. (b) Roma in Greek-style helmet as worn by Athena, (Roma's model) and by Britannia her successor. Wolf and twins on reverse.

new life was breathed into long-dead flans (Fig. 69). I know one collector who concentrates on *antoniniani*, less attractive at first sight than some other denominations but at the same time probably among the most obtainable. Inflation could be illustrated with representative silver and debased coins appropriately inserted into a coloured graph of the decline of silver.

Cheap as they are, it is suggested in several parts of this book that the small change of the fourth and fifth centuries offers a fascinating subject for thematic collecting. The mintmarks alone, together with the workshop and batchmarks of the larger mints, could be laid out quite attractively on a simple map of the Empire. Some rarer mintmarks take time to acquire.

The reverse designs furnish the vast majority of galleries in a collection. Augustus alone struck more than two hundred reverse types of his *denarii*. Personifications of virtues and abstract ideals, the Imperial family in various poses, animals, gods and goddesses afford plenty of theme choice. The collector interested in militaria might choose to collect the varieties of legionary standard ranging from the revered eagle through the ordinary standards (*signa* and *labara*) to what we might term 'the flag' (*vexillum*). The numbers and occasionally the titles of Rome's legions appear on a number of coins, some legions being scarcer and more in demand than others – because of their campaign

69. Earlier and later *sestertii*: (a) Augustus, struck posthumously by Nerva, AD 97. (b) Nero, *c.* AD 65. (c) and (d) Gallienus, AD 253–68.

associations. Troops themselves are shown on many coins in a variety of equipment issues over four centuries (Fig. 70).

Any one of Rome's provinces would make a readily encompassed theme for the enthusiast. *Britannia* might be the most obvious choice for an English-speaking collector but a memory of holidays spent in Jugoslavia, Spain, Greece or Turkey might prompt other equally interesting lines of pursuit.

Within the British theme, Carausius and Allectus allow for a natural self-contained subject confined to the space of a decade (see Ch. VIII). Their coinage is found in some profusion in Britain and the painstaking collector might be able to add to the growing body of knowledge about these coins which range from the badly executed and unflattering to fine silver *denarii* and impressive portraits. Scholars still discuss the puzzling 'Q-ship' issue of Allectus. Ships themselves make an interesting line to follow, from the basic Roman galley prow on the *asses* of the Republic to the many varieties of warship and merchant vessel shown on Imperial coins (Fig. 71). One Alexandrian variety shows the world's most famous lighthouse.

Buildings of all kinds abound on Roman reverses. They tend to be the more commonly found temples and commemorative arches (Fig. 72) but there are many variations on these as well as the rarer and very expensive views of the Circus, the Colosseum, the Port of Ostia and victory columns, all of which still stand either complete or in part in the vicinity of modern Rome. Their fame is enough to

70. The legions: (a) Legionary *denarius*, M. Antony, 32 BC, probably Ephesus mint. The title **LEG(io) VI** *Ferrata* is just visible beneath the standards. These coins circulated up to the mid-third century. Some legions are more sought after than others, e.g. **XVII, XVIII** and **XIX** which were wiped out in AD 9 in the German forests and the titles never used again (£12, 1980). (b) *Antoninianus*, Carausius, AD 287–93, struck for the **Cohors Pretoriana**, or the Imperial Guard and showing four standards (£480, 1981). (c) *Antoninianus*, Carausius, the ram badge of **LEG(io I) MIN(erva)** (£450, 1981). (d) Two fourth-century soldiers guard *labara* (standards) on a common coin from the Rome mint (from around £1 upwards, though not usually in this condition).

71. Ships: (a) Galley obverse of Mark Antony's legionary *denarius*. (b) Galley on a *denarius* of Hadrian. (c) Boat under wolf and twins on *denarius* of Domitian as Caesar, AD 77; possibly an allusion to the arrival of Aeneas from Troy by sea. (d) *Sestertius* of Trajan, the Danube bridge and beneath it the ferry, presumably redundant. It is also the artist's way of indicating water.

72. Buildings: usually depicted on the reverse of the larger and most sought-after coins. (a) Triumphal arch on a *sestertius* of Nero; the Stadium circus of Domitian on a *sestertius* of 'Caracalla', himself a racing fanatic. Both of these would cost several hundred pounds. (b) Within a budget collector's reach are these temples on coins struck by Antoninus Pius – the Temple of Venus and Rome, and the Temple of Faustina, still visible in Rome as the outer structure of the church of S. Lorenzo in Miranda in the Forum (£13 and £10, 1982). (c) A unique design showing the circular shrine of Juno Martialis, the first costing £2 in 1980 (Trebonianus Gallus) and the second being sold for £400 in 1981 (Volusian); the flan of each is curiously broken in exactly the same spot and in similar fashion.

command a price beyond the pocket of most collectors. The simple camp-gate reverse of the fourth century might make a theme more suited to many pockets (Fig. 73): the brickcourses vary in number and size; sometimes the gates are open, sometimes closed; the so-called 'turrets' (I suspect they are in fact beacons) range from two to four and may even have had some denominational significance in the early years of the design.

73. Permanent camp gates: (a) *Ae 3* or *centenionalis* of Constantine, **TR(everi) mint** (£1 each, 1981). (b) *argenteus*, Maximian, AD 304, **N(icomedia)mint** and half-*argenteus*, Constantine I, AD 307, **TR(everi) mint** (£100 and £720 respectively, 1981). The remains of such gates can be seen all over the Roman Empire.

Thematic collecting has taken some collectors well away from Roman Imperial coins. Egyptian products from the Alexandrian mint offer abundant material at good buying prices. Moving further east, some collectors are drawn to the Arab-Sassanian (Iranian) silver *drachmai* from the third to the seventh centuries AD, punched out onto fine broad flans, a novel and relatively inexpensive margin of the ancient market (Fig. 74).

Some collectors chase dates. Imperial coins are often dateable by terms of office (easily calculable thanks to the tables in Sear's handbook). Egyptian Roman coins simply have the year of the reign, almost modern by comparison. Other collectors follow stars and moons in the recurrent theme of astrology. The zodiac meant much to the people of the time and this is reflected even in the story of Christ's birth with its star and its Persian astrologer-priests or *magi*.

74. Late Sassanian-Arab silver *drachma*, broken, cracked yet remarkably clear despite age and fragility (£1, rummage tray, 1980).

Even the *Chi-Rho* 'Christogram' which appears on later Roman coins is a relic of the old sun religion – a curve is added to the top ray of a sunburst to form the Greek letter *Rho* stemming down through the crutch of the letter *Chi* (Fig. 75). The halo on the traditional picture of the saint stems back to the light behind the head of the sun-god (Apollo) and the rays on the Emperor's head on the *dupondius, antoninianus* and double-*sestertius*. It passed to the saints (who in turn replaced the range of Roman gods and goddesses) as it disappeared from the coins in the Christian period after the reign of Constantine. Similarly the stars and the crescent moon were transferred to images of the Virgin Mary who became in the popular mind a sort of heavenly *Diva Augusta* combined with the old roles of Juno, Venus and Diana (Fig. 76).

These are some suggested themes but they are only the tip of a berg. Others will occur to the collector quite naturally and further suggestions will be found in many articles and books. I hope that by shaking this book (metaphorically) a number of new themes will drop out on to the reader's lap.

75. Double-*centenionalis*, Magnentius, AD 350–3, **AMB(ianum) mint**, showing *Chi-Rho* with *Alpha-Omega* (see Fig. 49h).

76. (a) *Sestertius*, after AD 145, Antoninus Pius as the radiate sun. (b) 'Radiate' of Maximian, *c.* AD 295, one of the last to be issued. (c) *Antoninianus*, posthumous of Mariniana, issued by her husband Valerian after AD 253. Note the allusion to Juno through the peacock and the deification combined with the **consecratio**.

V

FORGERIES, FAKES AND COPIES

**An honest man tenders good (coins) out of his stock of
genuine ones while the forger tenders rubbish from his
bag of counterfeits. I tell you that every worthless word
which men utter they will have to account for at the final
reckoning.**

Matthew's Gospel, 12:35–6, *c.* AD 80

Some years ago a granite Roman pillar was uncovered near the River
Jordan. It carried a legionary inscription. A German professor of
archaeology interpreted it *in situ* as a monument set up by 'Engineers
of Legion LXXII *Colpica*, Monticola Albanica' (so ran the Latin
inscription), a hitherto unknown unit of the Roman army. Four months
after the discovery a retired Scottish brigadier explained (with a regret
tinged with unmistakable delight) that the pillar was genuine but the
inscription was made as recently as 1936 by the 1st Battalion (olim
72nd) Seaforth Highlanders, (Duke of Albany's Own), then serving a
tour in the Transjordan. Their colonel was a Latin scholar.

The pillar would hardly come under a major auctioneer's definition
of forgery, '*intended to deceive* as to authorship, date or provenance'. Forgeries and fakes do still challenge the professional and the small-time
collector should be no less aware of the hazard. There are many sorts
of copy. No reputable dealer would knowingly offer one as genuine
since it would be more than his name or business would be worth. The
major auctioneers cited above (Bonhams/Vecchi) guarantee against a
forgery being sold through their house, '*provided* that it is not shown
to be such in the catalogue description . . . that it was sold in accord
with the then generally accepted opinions of scholars and experts . . .
(and that) it can only be established as a forgery by processes not generally accepted for use (at the time of sale)'. With patience and observation (one dealer described it to me as 'a sixth sense which takes years
to develop') the collector can learn to avoid the pitfalls of the fake.
Forgery is a temptation as old as money. The law of Moses proscribes
it. Roman law was harsh in suppressing it. Even Jesus used it as an
illuminating metaphor from everyday life. In the same first century
Pliny Senior noted that forgers 'mix a bronze alloy for counterfeit
money' (*aera falsae monetae miscent*), presumably base core for plating.

Like their real counterparts, ancient forgeries have survived the test-punch, the merchant's teeth and the customer's attempt to break in two. The ear too is a good but not infallible guide to a 'dud'. In Italy in the 1960s there was a rash of forged 500 *lire* pieces. Most shops kept a marble tile on the counter and the coin proffered by a customer would first be tested for sound. Base metal utters a base note while the real article tends to 'sing'. On the other hand, the last of the debased third century *denarii* with only 40 per cent silver sound dull to the ear yet are still quite genuine.

Appearance offers certain clues. Cast marks may show on the edge of a 'coin' where molten metal has seeped into the hairline gap between the halves of the mould. In the case of an ancient moulded forgery it is worth remembering that time and wear may have removed both cast marks and the work of the finishing file. Also certain authentic coins such as the early Republican bronze and many eastern coins were struck onto pre-cast flans. There will have been no attempt to disguise the edge marks.

Old-fashioned casting also shows bubbles in the surface where air was trapped in tiny pockets. An uneven finish can sometimes be seen where the first metal into the mould cooled before the last or where the metal has stuck to the mould. A glass will show that these signs are quite distinct from the common pittings of time and corrosion (Fig. 77). Another sign might also be a too-perfect roundness, although it should be borne in mind that the mintmasters did aim for round coins and frequently came close to that ideal.

Weight is another indication which helps scholars to distinguish a dubious coin. Even here there can be a wide margin of error, due to bad alloying or inaccurate shearing at the mint. The crude base silver from Egypt under Nero sometimes drops to 9 gms and sometimes rises to 14 gms; the Jewish *lepta* under the Prefects vary from 1 gm to 2 gms, a 100 per cent margin of difference. However, if a forger were forging bronze in a time of inflation, such as the later third century, he would tend not to use the same quality or the same amount of bronze as the genuine model, otherwise he would be performing a non-profitmaking public service rather than engaging in lucrative crime.

Coiners' dens – whether forgers' such or semi-official is not always clear – have been found as far apart as Wales and Egypt. Sometimes their moulds in clay are offered for sale and make an interesting curio to add to a collection. Die-punches have also been found across Europe, notably in Spain and France. Britain's best known example is a reverse punch for either a *denarius* or *aureus* of Hadrian, now in the St Alban's museum. It may be official, unlike the reverse punch for a *denarius* of Crispina found in the north of England and offered for auction through Vecchi in 1981 (Fig. 78); it finally realised £800. A vast amount of work would be needed to match such dies to known coins. It has often been impossible to settle the argument as to whether they are forgers' instru-

77. Cast copy, *follis*, Diocletian. Note rough surface from the fired clay and the air bubble below the neck – injection moulding under pressure was then unknown. A worn coin has been the model for the mould but signs of real wear on the copy (as opposed to mirrored wear) are absent. The edge is too sharp. Genuine *folles* of the period are shown in different grades of preservation, for comparison (L–R) Maximian (×2), Diocletian.

78. (a) upper or punch die found in South Humberside, 1979. Venus on reverse matrix of a *denarius* of Crispina – almost certainly used for striking unofficial plated *denarii* (£800, 1981). (b) Impression.

ments or the real thing. Possibly some are both, stolen from a workshop or fashioned by an off-duty mint-worker.

Some coins are patent forgeries and cannot even be defended as 'semi-official' (Fig. 79). They still have their interest. Vecchi in 1981 also offered a forged Republican *denarius* in lead which may once have been silvered; it sold for half its estimate of £59. Forgery may have been banned by law but it seems to have been a thriving business. The Romans themselves were avid collectors. According to Pliny Senior

79. Base alloy 'barbarous' copy of a *denarius*, second-century type. The head was the crucial assay mark of Roman bullion; an illiterate legend would matter little to the majority of the population, because of either semi-literacy or language problems. The lightweight, cast flan has given way under pressure of striking.

'a specimen of a forged (*falsus*) *denarius* is much sought after and the counterfeit (*adulterinus*) article costs quite a number of real ones.' This may be one of the few instances of numismatic fever among the Romans themselves over their own coins. It is also worth noting that in a time of plentiful coin supplies – for example under Nero and in the Egyptian province up to AD 294 contemporary forgeries are almost unknown.

The forgery should not be confused with the 'contemporary copy', or even with the plated coin (see Ch. VI). 'Copies' abounded, for instance, after the Claudian invasion of Britain when there was a dearth of Imperial coin locally. They crop up throughout the western Empire in the grand debasement of the later third century when vast amounts of coins were needed to meet inflating prices. Unofficial (smaller) radiate-crowned *antoniniani* were struck. These copies tend also to be described as 'barbarous' which has unfortunately become accepted numismatic terminology.

These coins are contemporary copies to meet a need. It has been estimated that imitations far outnumbered official issues at certain times. They were either approved, suffered or even commissioned by the area administration. Some of Europe's earlier modern colonial money is of the greatest crudity – base metal and simple design would do for the natives. This is by no means always the case with so called 'barbarous copies', either of the Claudian period or of the third century. Claudian British copies range from the admittedly 'faintly reminiscent' (See Fig. 142b) right through to highly artistic renderings of the original Roman model (Fig. 80). Whatever their quality, they are genuine in the wider sense and, where they do approximate closely to the Roman die-cutter's portrait, they offer a bargain to the collector.

80. *Sestertii*, Claudius, AD 41–54: (a) Found in Britain and considered to be a good provincial copy (£18, 1979). (b) Imperial version which cost £300 in 1981. Both show **Spes** on whose feast day in AD 43 Claudius celebrated his fiftieth birthday.

The price drops once they are classed as 'copies', no matter that we know so little of their legal and manufacturing circumstances.

Real problems arise when we come nearer to our own time. The Italian Renaissance rediscovered, imitated and at times surpassed classical art, and coinage and medals were no exception. They made artistic copies of the fine material which was appearing from the ground. In fact, the studied roundness and flawless execution of these copies tends to betray their origin. Some are struck; some are cast; most have a fine finish and tend to have a uniform bronze patina. The edge of the design usually matches the edge of the flan too accurately. The flan itself is often the wrong size – too large for the *sestertius* and too small for the Roman medallion.

Material similar to the work of the Renaissance but lacking its quality and originality is sometimes found labelled as 'Paduan' or 'Paduan type'. The name derives from the Paduan school of medallists in Italy, notable among them Giovanni Cavino, which set much of the standard and the fashion for this imitative classical work in the sixteenth century. The more fantastic Renaissance pieces were probably never meant to deceive; their purpose was more to decorate or to entertain. In cases where a desirable *sestertius* or a rare medallion is directly imitated there may well have been profit motives behind the work. In fact, a genuine 'Paduan' commands a price in its own right simply as an example of Renaissance art. This is less true of later and paler imitations. Figure 81 gives a good example of a 'Paduan type' medallion. A fraction smaller than its original Roman model, it has been cast in good bronze with a fine finish; the obverse at least is a small work of engraving art. A micrometer would be needed to determine its date of execution, somewhere in the wide span between the sixteenth and twentieth centuries.

81. (a) Cast bronze copy of medallion of Commodus aged 18, AD 179. Probably eighteenth century. Due to loss in the casting process the copy is fractionally smaller than the originally struck medallion. (b) A contemporary *sestertius* of the young Commodus is shown below (£3, 'forged *sestertius*', 1980).

82. Edge of cast counterfeit coin, filed to hide the seam of the joined moulds and the stub(s) from the pouring channel(s).

In more recent centuries copies have been made of copies, particularly in the Mediterranean area. Usually the metal is wrong. The 'black museums' of major dealers contain, besides the expected brass '*aurei*', coppers made of good silver and even the unbelievable gold versions of coins struck originally only in silver. The more modern copy in bronze frequently has a crude varnish-like patina and patently faked pittings. They are too even to admit of ever having felt the striker's hammer. A 'soapy' feeling to the touch is a common giveaway. Generally they are too thin or too thick, too even and too large in diameter. Filed edges offer the most obvious clue (Fig. 82). These may have been buffed smooth but the resulting 'wear' has no corresponding 'wear' on the face of the coin. Filing also produces a sharp ridge, quite noticeable from the front of the piece. Only the very innocent are taken in by these tourist souvenirs. Occasionally the collector can use them to fill a gap (Fig. 83).

A vendor in Rome, Tripoli, Jerusalem or Ismir will always have a good tale to tell. The buyer is really paying a bard for his ballad. In Rome, each morning I used to pass an old man in the street corner selling paperweight-thickness (7 mm!) '*sestertii*' of Marcus Aurelius and bubbled brass '*asses*' of Galba, both with fine portraits. He gave the origin of this seemingly inexhaustible stock as 'a sealed amphora brought up from the bed of the river'. His finger would point with dramatic emphasis towards the unprotesting brown Tiber a few blocks away. Admittedly, much has come from the Tiber's protective silt –

83. (a) Cast copy of Tyrian *tetradrachmon*. (b) The real *tetradrachmon*. The cast of this popular fine silver coin with its biblical associations is shallower and less well defined than the genuine coin. The field is roughcast, while on the real coin it is overall smooth with fine striations.

but these certainly had not. Britain's museum curators often see such copies brought in for identifications and have to mete out the sad news to hopeful owners. It should be added that Mediterranean flea-markets do also have the genuine article, brought in by the workman and the farmer.

Even this holiday rip-off has its more sophisticated versions. Copies abound of the valuable *sestertii* of Gaius, Nero, Vitellius and Vespasian Today they are sometimes pressure-cast, thereby eliminating the tell-tale air bubbles but still omitting the tiny striations which only a hammer and punch produce. A brown 'patina', more like a burnish than a varnish is then induced but so evenly and taking away so little from the suspicious crispness of the coin that it gives itself away. A good rule of thumb to bear in mind is that today's caster-forger will only bother to cut a mould of the rarer coin or even the non-existent. Constantinian small bronzes are simply not worth forging, nor are pieces in the lower grades of condition. It is the well-preserved rarity which should be examined more closely. An interesting collection of rare bronzes of Otho can be built up but the collector should not be too depressed when he discovers that the Senate under Otho issued no Imperial bronze.

The electrotype copy (not to be confused with the silver and gold alloy called *electrum*, used by the Greeks) made in two halves, plated and given an artificial tarnish or tone can be more convincing. Museums sometimes sold them as facsimiles years ago. Those formerly sold by the British Museum carry an incuse initial on the rim. Others deceive the untrained eye until they are directly compared with the original. A buffed edge will show signs of a join; letters will be blurred in a way which is definitely not naturally induced wear; the tarnish will not come away easily; the electrotype is invariably lighter than the original. It may even be the case that it is a non-existent type of coin such as the '*argenteus*' of Crispus in Fig. 84, electrotyped in fact from a fairly common if attractive bronze.

a

b

84. (a) Electrotype, taken from a bronze of Crispus, Caesar AD 317–26, purporting to be an *argenteus* or *siliqua*. (b) A genuine bronze shown alongside, one of the last products of the London mint and costing £1 from a rummage tray, is a far more attractive item.

Verdigris, patina, pittings and even flan cracks can be imitated on forgeries with varying degrees of success. Perhaps the most easily recognised counterfeit is the one made of lead. It bends to finger pressure; a thin grey line can be drawn with its edge; it has no note when dropped and its weight and colour should give it away. There are a number of ancient lead forgeries in existence, perhaps appropriately since lead and silver tend to be mined together – ingots of lead are found marked as products of Imperial silver mines. A Republican law specified the lead counterfeit, condemning its fraudulent use but not its manufacture or its curio value which Pliny Senior suggests was considerable. Where these are found in a well or on a riverbed in some numbers there is reason to think that they were manufactured as votive offerings, ritual money to satisfy a deity rather than to fool the public. (Brass spade-guineas for Victorian card games may be an apt parallel.) Lead may also have been used to test out new dies and in extreme cases of shortage as part of a base silver alloy.

Figure 85 shows a mystery coin, purportedly from the Jewish Revolt and dated **Year Four**, (AD 69). It is a type known in the form of the bronze *prutah* (see Ch. VII) but here struck either in lead or a very base silver alloy. It may be a test-strike or even a last emergency issue struck as the Roman siege net tightened around Jerusalem. Above and to the right of the chalice is an incuse Latin letter **S**, similar to a test-mark or counterstrike. Two sides of the coin show that it has been broken from a pre-cast strip of flans as was customary in Syria and Palestine for the striking of base coinage. Faint traces suggest that it may once have been plated, or more accurately 'washed' with silver. One suggestion has been made that it is an emergency-issue one-eighth *shekel*. Some base metal issues are known from this period of the revolt, for instance sheklim in bronze. Whether rarity, fake or pious facsimile, the interesting fact remains that a bronze type has been reproduced apparently by striking in base white metal.

The best way around the pitfall of the false coin is to know what to

85. (a) 18 mm *prutah*-type of the Jewish revolt, AD 69, chalice of salvation twigs and fruit baskets. (£2, 'unwanted oddity', 1978). A senior member of Jerusalem's Hebrew University commented 'Somehow, it's too bad to be a forgery!' Pious facsimiles of Jewish coins are not uncommon. Note the letter **S** at nearly three o'clock. (b) A genuine *prutah* of Year Four is shown alongside.

86. Concave reverses of *sestertii*: (a) Domitian as Caesar, AD 77, Annona seated. (b) Macrinus, AD 217–18.

look for in the genuine article. All coins, but most noticeably the large *sestertius*, are just perceptibly 'bowled' on the reverse due to the downward pressure of reverse die and hammer (Fig. 86). This can, however, be reproduced on a good cast (see Fig. 83) and is part and parcel of the deception in a die-hammered copy. The genuine coin is usually unevenly centred, the die edge and coin edge forming eccentric arcs. The original hammered coin will tend to have an uneven level of profile or thickness since the angle of handheld die to flan could never be 100 per cent perfect. Under hammer pressure the metal also shows its flaws in the form of flan cracks and edge cracks. Fine striations appear on the surface from hammering but not from a mould. The relief, particularly the legend, should stand distinctly clear from the field with a clear crisp division between the two. Surface wear will be smooth and even – the fingers may interpret better than the eye. Real toning on silver will be removable, although it should be left alone. The edge of the coin will tend to be smooth, even pie-crusted at times as the edge has puffed out from the blow. There will, of course, be no mould traces on the edge or front of Imperial coins and usually no glitter from the older, genuine metal.

Forgery can be committed upon a genuine coin. It may be the subject of tooling where the patina is re-engraved either to improve the coin beyond recognition or to change a legend and design so that a rarity 'hitherto unpublished' is the end result. Valuable ancient restrikes such as Bar 'Kochba's' rebel *denarii* (see Ch. VII) are forged by taking the genuine but inexpensive *denarii* of the period and overstriking them with a counterfeit 'rebel' die. The Seaforth Highlanders played the same game with their Latin-inscribed pillar, but without the calculating malice to defraud.

As collecting has grown today, so too has the temptation to profit from sophisticated forgery of collectors's items. Plastic netsukes and mass-produced Iron Crosses are not untypical. All popular collector areas are potential minefields requiring a map, a detector and a wary eye. A regular bulletin of reported counterfeits is issued by the International Bureau for the Suppression of Counterfeit Coins. Its items read like newspaper scandals, as indeed they are: 'Trajan Decius expert strikes again!' or 'Jugoslavian "*sestertii*" still appearing!' Silver and gold are now the most frequently forged pieces in all types and periods of coin. Hammered coins are even being struck with properly engraved dies, although minute gravure lines on the field give their newness away. In some cases, toughened plastic dies and plastic moulds help to create a finer finish.

Experience is the best instructor. Leading museums even hesitate to pronounce on some items. The law also protects since it is an offence knowingly to offer a forged ancient coin with intent to deceive. It cannot be stressed too often that no self-respecting dealer would pass on such items without proper description. On the whole the dealer should be given .credit for honesty while trying to make a profitable living. Some even keep their own 'black museum', one way of preventing fraudulent material from going back into circulation. The collector would be wise to keep his receipt or numbered coin envelope after purchase and in the last resort, if he feels dissatisfied and if a fake has passed even the dealer's experienced eye, the item can be returned. The vendor will be only too glad to take it back and to keep both the customer's trust and his own good name.

VI

MYSTERIES OF THE MINT

What is it that spurs (the trader) to face all those hardships and perils? Silver, stamped out in tiny roundels with portraits and superscriptions!

Juvenal, *Satire* XIV, *c.* AD 130

History and techniques

The Roman mint (and thereby the words themselves, *money* and *mint*) originated by the Temple of Juno Moneta on the Capitol, a secure and easily guarded spot. It occupied the Temple precinct along with Rome's measurement standards for some three centuries. Juno features on some Republican *denarii* together with the tools of the mint-worker. The tourist can still visit the site, Rome's heat and his legs permitting the haul, up a steep stairway into the present church of S. Maria in Ara Caeli – Mary took Juno's role and temple as Queen of Heaven. A serious fire damaged the mint in the second half of the first century AD and by the reign of Trajan (AD 98–117) production was housed by the baths which bore his name. Possibly this rehousing is commemorated by the huge and still frequently encountered issue of *Moneta Augusti* coins under Domitian (Figs 66 and 87).

The Romans regarded the coin as a quasi-religious item, presumably embodying something of what it represented. *Pecunia* and *moneta* were almost invariably *sacra*. The Byzantine ikon and the Moslem reaction against it was in the same tradition, as were the touchpieces and 'lucky coins' of more modern times. Occasionally a coin commemorated not simply *moneta* but all three major metals of currency, the *tres monetae*, each Junoesque figure shown with a pile of coin at her feet. The Roman family which actually venerated a sacred *triens* was regarded as quite exceptional, even by Pliny Senior. They were said to have provided offerings of silver and gold which were then promptly gobbled up by the pampered little bronze. Given that Pliny checked out his facts and the story is more than just *ben trovato*, even today's most addicted collector cannot match such enthusiastic respect.

Under Augustus and Tiberius, Imperial gold and silver seems to have been struck at Lyons. Bronze, mintmarked **SC** by the Senate,

a   b

87. (a) *As*, Domitian, AD 86, Juno Moneta with scales. These coins were issued from AD 84; since the Capitol was largely destroyed by fire in AD 80, the coin type may mark a relocation of the mint. (b) *Follis*, Constantius I, **AQ(uileia)** mint, AD 301, with the same design, proclaiming the new monetary policy of the tetrarchs. Aquileia was one of the new mints opened some six years previously (£2 and £65, 1979.)

continued to be made at Rome. The Lyons mint had a military guard, not unlike the Bank of England until recent years. Presumably security in general was high. After at least half a century in Lyons, the Imperial mint for precious metals was recentred in Rome, possibly in Gaius 'Caligula's' time, possibly considerably later. We do not know whether it joined the Senatorial mint under the shadow of Juno Moneta. Lyons, either in unbroken continuity or opened anew, produced much of Nero's great coinage of AD 64 and minted in all metals, at least until the time of Titus (AD 79–81). Times of disturbance, as for instance under the 'Gallic Emperors' or the British usurpers of the third century saw the founding of regional mints. By the end of the third century the number of regional mints had grown to the point where Diocletian simply felt compelled to formalise the reality. Across the Empire he imposed uniform standards of design and compulsory mint identification marks.

Mintmarks of some kind had their place throughout the whole period of Roman coinage as a form of quality control: rogue work can be traced back to its source. In the earlier days of the Republic they also afforded a way to personal advancement. Moneyer's initials appear in the second century BC. Names and 'canting' (punning) designs on those names appear on later Republican *denarii* (see Fig. 95). A board of three moneyers was responsible for mint matters, entitled in short **III VIRI AAA FF** (Fig. 88). Commanders in the field (*Imperatores*) and *Praefecti* of fleets and cities had traditional rights to strike for their own use. Mark Antony, Octavian, Pontius Pilatus and the Prefect of Alexandria all struck money as of ancient right. The new position of emperor, carved out diplomatically by Augustus from his military supremacy, simply inherited that right. Lyons probably began as a field mint.

88. *As*, Augustus, 7 BC, showing title **III VIR AAA FF** and the moneyer's name Maecilius Tullus. **Tres Viri, auro, argento, aeri, flando feriundo** = three man board for the shaping and striking of gold, silver and bronze. Flat-struck (see Fig. 50).

Handbooks commonly say that mintmarks only appear in the third century. This is not quite true. The **S**(*enatus*) **C**(*onsulto*) retained on all Imperial bronze for nearly three hundred years is in fact a senatorial mintmark. Understandably it faded out as the usurper emperors of the frontiers struck their own coins, thousands of miles away from the Senate. It became as nominal as is the Papal honour **Fid. Def.** on modern British coins. In the first century of empire, however, it was more than a formality: the Senate seems to have ordered the melting down of the coins of Gaius 'Caligula', but only the bronze; forty years later the same body managed to withhold from Otho the issue of base metal currency. Once the collector understands the exceptions, he will find the **SC** mark useful as a guide to distinguishing Imperial coinage in bronze from both provincial and medallion pieces.

The names of the three-man board of moneyers died out on coin in about 4 BC. Publicly comprehensible mintmarks did not appear again till the third century. But there are grounds for believing that there were secret or 'privy' mintmarks, much more than simple differences in artistry, which gave those in the know the workshop and the location. For example, the position of the wreath ties could indicate this. Variations upon and breakpoints in the legend could also provide coded information. The case has been argued strongly for Alexandrian workshops in the first three centuries of empire – it may apply across the board.

A better-known mark is the 'globe' at the tip of the neck on the western (believed to be Lyons) issues of Nero and the Flavians (Fig. 89). It may also be a mark of outlying mints in Spain. In the present century British pennies of George V were struck in Birmingham as well as London, carrying a distinguishing initial under the neck

89. So-called 'globe' (in fact a legend stop) on coins of Nero and the Flavians, the mark of a western mint, believed to be Lyons. The exaggerated stop-mark became a mint characteristic.

of the bust. Some mints in AD 296 maintained the custom of a distinguishing artistic mark: the large *follis* issue depicting the Genius of the Roman People was uniform throughout the Empire in the early fourth century, save for the products of the ancient, traditional mints such as Lyons and Alexandria (Fig. 90). Once the collector has an idea of the workings of the mint and its limitations, he can then understand and judge his coins better. His imagination can also have free rein with certain coins as to what time or what sense of humour may have marked their striking. He may also start to look out for oddities and 'escapees' from the mint.

Doubtless there was a ruling that dies be kept under tight security and destroyed at the end of their useful life. This may explain why so few have been found. Usually it is the upper (*trussel* or *punch*) die which has survived, the reverse design. It is not always easy to tell which die is genuine and which is forger's concoction. Possibly some forgers were mint-trained. Common sense also suggests that the upper die would have been easier to pocket and steal. It had a shorter life than the anvil (*staple* or *pile*) die, due to wear from the hammer blows. Even hardened bronze dies appear to have had an iron sheath for longer wear, as in the case of the St Alban's die. They would have been discarded and replaced more frequently than their opposite number in the anvil recess. Hammering the upper die into the flan produced a slight concave effect, probably reinforced by a slight bevel on the die-surface itself. The obverse of most coins is in higher relief – as the more important side it was also entrusted to the more skilled design-cutter.

a   b   c

90. Although the mints were regulated under Diocletian's reforms of AD 294–6, the die cutters added local detail to mark the older mints; e.g. the Genius *folles* for the most part show the simple figure (a). (b) Some of those at Lyons add an altar as formerly featured on the older Genius patterns of the first century. Alexandria (c) adds the Ptolemaic eagle from the days before the Roman Empire.

We know a certain amount of the minting technique from monumental carvings showing workshop, workers and tools. The diagram of the workshop process (Fig. 91) suggests a team of workmen much akin to the group which puts together a modern car. A master-engraver, possibly a Greek who had bought his freedom, at least in Rome, supervised a team of slave die-cutters rather like craft apprentices. Some probably never graduated. The less able may have done the lettering after a skilled artist incised the relief.

There is good reason to link the engraving of coin dies with the cutting of intaglio gemstones, usually for rings. In the case of Roman Imperial gems, the work is almost always mirror or negative incision, presumably with a view to impressing wax-seals. One common example from the turn of the first century, when both intaglio and coin-die engraving seems to have reached a peak of craftsmanship in Rome, is the pair of clasped hands – on coins denoting the support of the army for the Emperor, on ringstones a symbol of marriage. Another common link is found between the perched eagle of Jupiter, usually a posthumous reference on **Consecratio**-type coins, and gems showing the same invoking the patronage of Jupiter over the wearer (Fig. 92).

The artists were supplied by smelters and smiths who poured molten metal into open moulds after alloying and who hammered out sheets and strips after cooling. Trim men, sometimes apparently contract workers, cut out the shape of the flan with varying degrees of success. A hammerer with good muscles struck the upper die into the heated flan placed on the anvil die, presumably with tongs and in a small recess to prevent its slipping. Another worker, also armed with tongs, held the upper die to the flan as if steadying a chisel while the hammer was lifted and dropped. It was hot work. Like the shell-packers of the First World War they were probably hard drinkers. A back-up staff may have provided refreshment. There were certainly accountants of one sort or another, while a works foreman supervised the whole workshop, at least at 'blue collar' level.

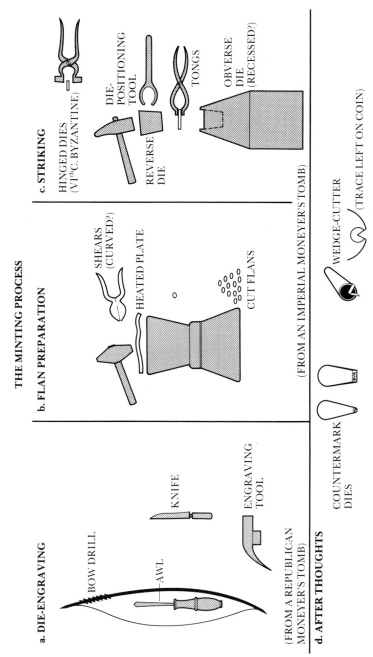

THE MINTING PROCESS

a. DIE-ENGRAVING

BOW DRILL

AWL

KNIFE

ENGRAVING TOOL

(FROM A REPUBLICAN MONEYER'S TOMB)

b. FLAN PREPARATION

SHEARS (CURVED?)

HEATED PLATE

CUT FLANS

(FROM AN IMPERIAL MONEYER'S TOMB)

c. STRIKING

HINGED DIES (VIᵗʰC. BYZANTINE)

DIE-POSITIONING TOOL

REVERSE DIE

TONGS

OBVERSE DIE (RECESSED?)

d. AFTER THOUGHTS

COUNTERMARK DIES

WEDGE-CUTTER

(TRACE LEFT ON COIN)

91. Diagram of the workshop process in the Roman mint.

92. Intaglio gem, *c.* AD 100, eagle on altar (8 × 10 mm). (a) Surface scuffing hinders a clear view of the design. (b) Impression. (c) *Denarius*, Vespasian, AD 76 and posthumous *antoninianus*, Claudius Gothicus, *c.* AD 270.

East and west employed different striking techniques. In Pilatus' mint at Caesarea Maritima, the small Jewish bronzes were first cast in a row of bevelled flan-moulds. These were joined together by a thin channel to facilitate pouring. The break-off points from this connecting strip of metal can be seen clearly on many eastern coins, on opposite sides of the coin edge (Fig. 93a). The edges of Alexandrian coins (save for the silver) are similarly bevelled but without the break-off points – the Egyptian moulds appear to have been individual, not connected in line (Fig. 93b). A great number of bronze coins from the east carry a hubmark in the centre of both obverse and reverse. This indentation,

93. (a) Ptolemaic bronze and Herodian *lepton*; note the remains of the connecting strip formed in the pouring channel of a line of open moulds; the bevelled edges come from the bowl-shape of the mould. (b) *Ae* 35 mm, *drachma*, Alexandria, Hadrian, showing the bevel-edged product of the flan mould but without the connecting strip.

not found on western coins, is believed by some to be caused by the centring points of some kind of lathe used in finishing the edge of the flan. It may even result from a centering point on the die itself. Imperial *sestertii* of the second and the third centuries were struck on flans sheared from strips, sometimes so crudely that they are almost square (see Fig. 62).

The coins themselves reveal many of these techniques as well as their imperfections. I have a common 'Q-ship' issue of Allectus minted in London. On the edge of the flan there seems to be a tong-snip from poor handling of the heated metal in the workshop. Such snips are quite common in later third-century coins and allow us at least to measure the width of the tongs used (Fig. 94, see also Fig. 63b). Other coins show vibration marks, similar to double vision, resulting from double-striking or a repeated hammer blow which has caused the die to jump a fraction away from its first position.

Even the hardened bronze dies wore while still in use producing 'worn' coins before circulation. They also became fouled with metal from previous strikes like a typewriter letter which has not been cleaned. Fouling (and rust in the case of iron dies) would disfigure the legend or design and even embed itself in the heated metal of the flan: this is noticeable in some silver issues. A fire at the mint in Rome or Lyons would produce plenty of water to rust iron dies, just as much as storage in some damp workshop. The first few strikes of the day would then bring the rust out into the flans.

Some other tool, presumably a punch, seems to have been used to cut a wedge shape out of the edge of certain coins. This can be confused with a flan crack. The cut may have been to prevent their becoming legal tender, prevent their leaving the mint or even, as the many wedge-cut coins found in the recent Bath excavations suggest, to convert them from secular to religious use. The cuts are curiously uniform in size and not uncommon. In my experience they occur on flawed coins, quite distinct from flan cracks. Perhaps in religion the Romans were as irreverent (or realistic) as the twentieth-century soldiers in garrison

94. Tong-snip on a galley-issue '*quinarius*' of Allectus, AD 293–6, a common feature of later third century coins due to careless handling of a heated flan. The width of the tongs used in the London mint matches exactly those in use in Cologne some thirty years before (see Fig. 63b). (Found in road-works, Chichester, 1974).

churches who used to place brass buttons in the collection plate. We do know they burgled temples. Lead '*denarii*' seem to have been good enough for Father Thames. In the same vein, flawed coin might do for Sulis Minerva. After all, she never spat them back.

There are other marks which do not come from the mint. Moneyers in the cities gave out new issues just as does the bank today. They inflicted testmarks for plating on many silver and gold coins – the test sometimes failed to break good plate (Fig. 95). The mark might be a tiny circle, a hubbed or quartered circle or simply a letter. Bronze would not usually need testing, but at times the base metal coin did fail to come up to standard: forgers sometimes plated iron with orichalcum or cast lightweight *asses*, particularly in Britain; genuine *sestertii* and *dupondii* were also released from the mint with badly mixed alloy, appearing today as either dark rivers of copper or small beads of corrosion in the surface, the remains of copper globules (see Fig. 58).

The names and personalities of the workshop sections escape identification. Unlike the élite Greek artists who signed the giant *dekadrachmon* pieces of Syracuse, the Roman did not sign his masterpieces, at least to our present knowledge. Perhaps it was because he was a slave. In fact, the names of few Roman artists have come down to us, save for the occasional gem-cutter or the humble potter. Yet there are still signs of the men at work. No two dies are alike. A painstaking scholar can trace a style through a working life of engraving – perhaps thirty years. Some cutters had problems of language and give away their origin at least, if not their names. The Hebrews working in Pilatus' mint, for instance, executed poorly-formed Greek letters and at times in ungrammatical sequence. At Alexandria, even if they were Greek-speaking, they had spelling and grammar problems. Poppaea is called **sebastou** and **sebasté** (*Augusti* and *Augusta*) while the **b** in the basic word is sometimes doubled. In Rome under Nero when Greek artists were brought in for the new wave of coin, some betrayed their

95. *Denarius*, Republic, 48 BC, C. Vibius Pansa moneyer, supporter of Julius Caesar. The bust of Pan is a play on the moneyer's name. Testmarks **E** and **S** are still visible (£0.75, 1965). Worn Republican *denarii*, treasured for their fineness, circulated in Britain to the time of Hadrian, particularly in the (more traditional?) north. Analysis of finds shows that around AD 107, Trajan called in Republican silver save for the legionary issues of Mark Antony which may have been regarded as baser than they actually were (see Fig. 70).

96. *As*, Nero, *c.* AD 66, Genius of the Emperor and altar. Note the Roman **V** cut as a Greek **Y** (£1, 1978).

origin by rendering the Roman **U** not as a **V** but as its equivalent Greek **Y** (Fig. 96). Varied spellings occur on the London issues from Carausius to Constantine, not to mention illiteracies and figures mismatched with legends, almost invariably on the less skilfully cut reverse. Curiously, the name Carausius itself is rarely misspelt although it is a challenge to today's typist, let alone a third-century cutter. They even had problems with the quality control mark. For example, **DLN** is quite clear on a *follis* of Maximinus, a mistaken interpretation of a compacted **P** on another die or model (Fig. 97).

Each mint workshop must have had its bad engraver or striker with a reputation among his colleagues. Other mints besides Alexandria must have taken on seasonal unskilled labour at peak periods, much as the British Post Office hires students to cope with Christmas deliveries. Misspellings and flaws in legends further seem to confirm the belief that the letter engravers were not in the same skilled class as the design-cutters; likewise less skilled artists seem to have been relegated to do the reverse dies. As in the Victorian office, there must have been a social pecking order. Work will also have slipped below standard as the day and then the week slowed down to its close.

Did the workers laugh at the subject of their designs? The *dupondius* in Fig. 102 suggests that there may have been humourists at work. It is a matter of record that the bull on Julian's restored *folles* was the target of some mockery. Surely they must have made ribald jokes about

97. Reduced *follis*, Maximinus II, London mint between AD 309–13. Note blundered mintmark, **DLN** in place of **PLN** (£9, 1981).

the horn protruding from Elagabalus' forehead or the length of Maximinus' chin matching his reputedly seven-foot body. It is hard to
believe that Nero's flab, Otho's toupee and Domitian's early baby-face
passed through the workman's hands without comment.

Countermarks

These are either abbreviations or symbols punched into the design of
a coin after minting, usually some time after circulation has begun.
They add greatly to the interest of a piece. Sunk below the surface,
they may be in better condition than the rest of a worn coin. In many
cases they were actually marks to prolong the life of worn currency.
Reheating and counterstriking tend to leave the other side flattened
and slightly distorted.

The countermark would have required a special punch die. Sometimes the impact of the countermarking has bent a coin. Almost invariably the reverse of the coin has been flattened due to reheating
and then striking against a flat anvil top. Tong or pincer marks are frequently discernible. The minute detail in some countermarks suggests a
use of magnifiers. The lens was certainly known to the ancients. Jewel-
ler's rock crystal made a natural enlarger; bookworms used glass vessels
of water; Nero even had 'emerald' racing glasses. Eyestrain was still
probably a hazard of engraving.

Besides extending the life of a coin as legal tender, countermarks
served other purposes. Some extend the area of circulation. Some
appropriate the coin to local or to special military use. Others inform
of the accession of a new emperor and in rare cases seem to take the
place of a coin die itself on an otherwise blank flan. Many of the eastern
countermarks from the second and third centuries are indecipherable
but can still make a fascinating collection at little expense. Sometimes
they re-tariff a coin. Occasionally they are a traditional mark added
to stress a proud city origin such as Corinth. In some cases they might
even have been a control agent against forgery – like our metal strip
in the banknote.

A fairly worn *sestertius* of Claudius carries the countermark **PROB**,
thought to stand for *probatus* (approved). Nero recalled much coinage,
replacing it in AD 64 with new and more artistic work. The worn and
semi-official coins in circulation served Rome's image badly but some
of the more recently struck pieces were still acceptable twenty years
after they had been struck (Fig. 98). Another stamp on a Claudian
sestertius, **NCAPR**, has been interpreted in the same way, *Nero Claudius
Augustus Probavit*, serving the same purpose as **PROB**. A more attractive interpretation was offered by the late Keeper of the Ashmolean's
coins – *Nero Claudius Augustus Populo Romano* (to the Roman People).
The suggestion is that the coin was part of the largesse given out by

the Emperor on his accession along with bounty to his troops. A modern equivalent would be a combination of a Coronation medal, a Maundy Money case and the Christmas bonus for pensioners. However, other countermarks reading only **NCAP** make this reading less likely (Fig. 99).

The army had its own stamps. This dated back to the old right of field commanders to strike for their needs. During and after a major campaign troops would have to be paid. At times the pay might have to be in locally appropriate currency. After the four-year Jewish campaign, Palestinian coins were counterstruck by Legions VI *Ferrata* and X *Fretensis* (See Fig. 12). The paymaster's chest in some theatres of war must have been as assorted as a button box. When, on pay parade, the troops saw their own regimental countermark, they would presumably have felt more confidence that they were not being short-changed.

Nîmes in France issued a double-busted coin of Augustus and Agrippa, known from its reverse as the 'crocodile bronze'. It was struck at this *colonia* of ex-sailors for over thirty years, possibly even longer. The coin had a circulation well beyond Nîmes itself. The name **NEM**

98. *Sestertius*, Claudius, AD 41–54, countermarked **PROB**. There was a shortage of coin during Claudius' reign: many coins were copied locally and orichalcum coins were even struck in iron with a brass cladding. The reverse is flattened by re-heating and re-striking (Roman workman).

99. *Sestertius*, Claudius, AD 41–54, countermarked **NCAPR**. It could be a donative as mentioned in Suetonius (*Claudius* 7 and 11). The reverse, **Ob Cives Servatos** is legible but flattened by the process. (£2, 1973).

(ausus) denotes an Imperial mint rather than a mere local capital. One countermark on the Nemausus *as* is the palm branch and **DD**. It may be an early extension of the coin's use by decree of the local magistrates, hence **D(ecreto) D(ecurionum)**. The victory palm may be the badge of a naval *colonia* settlement. On the other hand it may mark a piece of largesse, an anniversary issue to mark the naval engagement at Actium, hence **D(onum) D(edit)**. The yellow metal and the size of the coin make me wonder whether it is a value mark, tariffing the coin as an international *dupondius* (Fig. 100).

The variety of countermarks from the east is endless. They can be picked up very cheaply from rummage trays and are at the moment something of a blind spot in scholarly research. They also offer hours of amusement to the puzzle enthusiast. One extreme might be the worn copper with three countermarks (Fig. 101a). Another might be the blank flan with a miniature bearded emperor's head and what appear to be three letters (Fig. 101b). Others come from cities which boast the cult statue of their local deity in miniature – Diana of Ephesus, Artemis of Lydia (Fig. 101c). In fact it is worth looking closely at even the most

100. '*As*' of *Nemausus* (Nîmes), Augustus (R) and his admiral Agrippa (L), *c.* 20–10 BC, countermarked **D D** and palm branch (£2, 1979).

a   b   c

101. (a) Worn *assarion* (?Antioch?) with three countermarks, presumably two letter-numerals and a symbol, either a revaluation or a date (£0.50, 1979). (b) Six-millimetre countermark of bearded head (Imperial? or a deity?) and three letters, the last being **X**. The apparently blank flan seems to have the remains of another countermark, this time much more shallow and very worn (£0.20, 1981). (c) Artemis of Lydia, countersunk into an *Ae 32 mm* of Lydia under 'Caracalla', AD 211–17 (£120, 1981).

corroded coin since 'damage' can turn out to be officially inflicted marks of great interest.

This is not the place to discuss the unofficial marks (see Ch. III) but it should be noted that in times of persecution in the second and third centuries, Christians sometimes used coins as pass tokens, presumably into domestic gatherings. A coin might be incised with a homespun *Chi Rho graffito* or a fish somewhere in the field, carefully avoiding defacement of the Imperial bust or reverse design.

Curiosities of the mint

In our own day British coins of the uncrowned Edward VIII are known to have escaped the mint, as did some of George V's 'non-existent' 1933 pennies. British 50p pieces have been found struck with the dies of a commemorative crown – the result looks more like a Roman than a twentieth century mis-strike.

I have a *dupondius* of Antoninus Pius, struck twice on the reverse with two different dies of the same year, **TR POT XXI** (Fig. 102). The ladies (one appears to be Annona) stand at 180° to each other, giving a playing-card effect. The obverse shows vibration from the second strike. A wedge of 'ritual killing' or quality disapproval (see Ch. III) has been cut into the edge. On the reverse, punchmarks like a banker's tests have been inflicted for good measure. It may have been the result of a sense of humour or an idle moment one lunchtime in AD 157. More probably it was a testpiece on which they tried out as many tools as possible – three dies, a wedge-cutter and a testpunch. It may have been kept as a novelty, hence the condition of the obverse.

102. *Dupondius*, Antoninus Pius, AD 157. The obverse shows the vibration from double-striking; the reverse shows two distinct figures; **TR POT XXI** is repeated, but with different breaks. It has been testmarked at two o'clock and wedge-cut at eight o'clock (£2, 1979).

The overstrike is not uncommon. It often met an emergency. Carausius' first coins were struck on inverted portraits of older *antoniniani*. The Jewish rebel, Simon Bar 'Kochba', used Roman flans quite plainly overstruck with Jewish designs (see Fig. 126). Ready-made flans in recognisable denominational sizes save an usurper time, expense and disruption in the rush to coin for a new situation. In AD 67–70 the rebels in Jerusalem used some of the vast number of bronzes struck by Procurator Felix under Nero to make their own Hebrew *prutot* (see Fig. 124a). Postumus, the usurper in Germany, Gaul and Britain, coined fine round *sestertii* and double *sestertii* on older flans (see Figs 61b and 63). It made economic sense. It also meant in the latter case that the *sestertius* as well as its publisher went out with a bang rather than a whimper. Half an hour with a glass on certain coins to establish their pedigree might be well rewarded.

A slightly amusing effect is caused on an *as* of Claudius where two different dies have been used (Fig. 103). *Libertas* has been overstruck onto the figure of *Constantia*. The flatstriking allows us to see part of the original reverse. *Libertas* has taken on an extendable four-boned arm and the mintmark reads **SSC**.

I have already touched upon the language problems of the die-cutting fraternity. Perhaps pressure caused 'howlers' to be passed by quality control. Perhaps the mintmaster had language problems, too. In the days before rules of language were strictly formulated, variations in grammar and even in letter formation were part and parcel of a living language. **Tethicus** may not be a misspelling of **Tetricus** at all, but an acceptable local version of an **R**. Variations in the word **Tranquillitas** on small bronzes of Constantine are more easily explicable as abbreviations forced on the engraver by lack of space. In fact, irregu-

103. *As*, Claudius, *c.* AD 45, (local copy?); **Libertas Augusta** (Imperial freedom) overstruck onto **Constantia Augusti** (the Emperor's courage) (£6, 1981).

larities in general are easier to understand in the case of local coinages from Palestine, Egypt and Britain. It is far harder to understand in the case of a fine, almost medallic *sestertius* issued under Domitian at Rome itself. Did it come to the Emperor's notice that one of his victory *sestertii* had been struck **GERMANIA CATPA!**? (Fig. 104). How did he react? A mint supervisor may have suffered for such a dangerous mistake under this megalomaniac. The condition of the piece may just be due to the fact that it is was kept and prized just as a philatelic error might be today. More prized, then just as much as today, would have been the *brockage* coin, where the relief design on one side is backed by the same design incuse. These examples could be produced by human error, where a striker failed to notice that a previous coin had stuck to the die and proceeded to hammer the newly struck piece into a new blank flan. They could also be produced deliberately as the illustration in Fig. 105 might suggest.

Plating

The puzzle of the plated *denarius* has already been raised. Through sheer force of numbers these coins cannot be ignored by collectors, even

104. *Sestertius*, Domitian, AD 86, marking German victory. Note the reverse misspelling **CATPA** (£375, 1978).

105. Obverse brockage, *sestertius* of Tiberius, AD 22, marking his aid to eastern cities after violent earthquakes. The **SC** is normally on the reverse and has here been transposed to the obverse, suggesting that this may be a deliberate presentation piece rather than human error ($1,500 upwards, American auction estimate, 1982).

if scholars are unable to resolve their exact pedigree. The quality and low price of some of them make them collectors' bargains.

Plating is first found in the Republic in the late second century BC. Later Republican *denarii* were actually serrated for a time in an attempt to convince the public of their silver content. (In more critical times Mark Antony the *triumvir* 'added base metal (*ferrum*) to his *denarius*'. Pliny, however, exaggerated this debasement since Antony's legionary *denarii* are about 85 per cent fine. Still in circulation two centuries later and common enough today, they have proved as tough as iron.)

Under Augustus and Tiberius a flood of plating seems to occur, unless the examples we encounter are survivors by natural selection from the melting campaigns. The plating is good and the artwork as good as that of the silver coinage proper (Fig. 106a). Testmarks sometimes appear in discreet spots though they often fail to break through the plate. Once the surface was broken the coin lost more and more of its silver. Some coins are even deliberately bent to test-break them for silver.

106. Plating. (a) *Denarius*, Augustus, *c.* 25 BC, Italy. Two arches marking Actium were built, one at Brindisi and one at Rome. Augustus rides a quadriga: the cutter evidently right-handed, has miscalculated the space for the first (last on the die) horse! A tiny testmark on the chin has failed to break the heavy plate. Testmarks were discreet – to allow the coin to be passed on even if it failed? (£10, 1980). (b) Plated *denarius*, Severus, AD 193–211, from Britain. The thin plate is of poor quality (£1, 1980). (c) *Antoninianus*, Gordian III, AD 238–44, heavily plated and showing the copper core in patches. The coin was only re-introduced in the year of his accession. (d) *Antoninianus* of Gallienus, AD 253–68, from late in his reign. The silver 'pickling' is so poor that it is not usually found intact (£1, 1979). (e) *Follis*, Maximian, *c.* AD 300, **Section 2 T(icinum) mint** with much of its plating still intact (£22, 1981). (f) Later base billon coin of Constantine, with traces of plate around the **V**, protected by the rim of the inner circle (£0.50, 1980).

From time to time hoards of plated first-century *denarii* make their way on to the market. They may have been counterfeiters' stocks, (the 'bag of counterfeits' in Matthew 12?) ready for slow release to the public. They may have been financiers' rejects. They may also be the last of their kind. After the first century it is more difficult to see the point of making plated *denarii*, if in fact it was still (or even *ever*) an official process. Silver was being debased. The thinner, almost tin plating of later second-century *denarii*, heralding the silver 'pickling' on the worst of the later *antoniniani*, quickly betrays the base core: even the sound of the coin when dropped is duller and flatter than the relatively healthy note uttered by a plated Augustan coin (Fig. 106b).

It took skill to make a pair of dies, then to plate the flan effectively and strike a successful coin. As the currency was debased, the time and effort involved became less worthwhile. In fact, the leaden dullness of much later plating, the semiliterate lettering and shoddy artwork suggest an unofficial production line close to outright forgery.

The earlier plated coin may have been made to fill gaps in available currency. The later ones may have been forgeries. Possibly the so-called earlier ones were later forgeries put on to a market wary of Nero's debased silver. One ingenious theory is that slaves in the mint were always looking for extra cash for daily life or to put towards a freedom purchase. By producing plated coins and passing them into circulation, they could steal silver from the allocation for themselves. Pliny Senior has an interesting aside: 'some (unspecified) short-measure the weight, even though law demands that eighty-four *denarii* be stamped out from a pound (of silver)'. The slave near the production of money must have been tempted in this direction. Some of the platings may even be the work of 'moonlighting' slaves, off duty and working simply as unusually skilled forgers. The modern tag 'black economy' may be particularly appropriate given the colour and condition of some of their 'silver' products.

There are interesting parallels to the two phases of plated *denarius*. In the third century, Gordian III issued plated *antoniniani* in bulk (Fig. 106c). A few years later, at the eye of the inflation storm, Gallienus simply 'pickled' (by reheating and immersion in salts) *antoniniani* with a minimal silver content and released the mean end-products onto the public (Fig. 106d). Again, at the beginning of the fourth century, the new large *follis* carried a trace of silver and was quite well plated (Fig. 106e). Two decades later the *follis* had suffered drastic reduction in size and its poor silvering survives in tiny grey patches only, if at all (Fig. 106f).

The portraits

How did the Imperial portraits come to be copied so faithfully, Empire-wide, so quickly after accession? Perhaps the images were sent literally post haste, via the Imperial posting stations along those major roads for which Rome became famous. The system provided an express delivery for government officials and packets and a burden at times crippling for the taxpayer. It also tended to be overused and abused by civil servants and their later counterparts, the Christian bishops. A rare *sestertius* of Nerva marks his legislation removing the cost of this service from the Italian citizen at least (see Fig. 15b).

Certainly some standard portrait seems to have been issued as one of the first acts of a reign. Legions carried the Imperial portrait on their standards and because of the key place of the legions in the emperors' position of power, these images changed even more promptly than the brass buttons and badges of some British Army regiments in 1936, the 'Year of the Three Kings'. It has even been suggested that coin dies were made centrally and then issued abroad, at least in the first century of empire. The question is more important for the first three centuries than the later period when stylised icons seem to portray offices rather than personalities.

The renderings of Nero are not identical but they all seem to stem from a similar basic model. The earlier Nero smacks much more of Claudius than of the heavily jowled young man of AD 64 struck in Rome, Lyons or Egypt (see Fig. 115). In AD 68–9 four emperors filled a year. Many dies must have been jettisoned before their useful life was over. Old reverses were married to new portraits. Countermarks quickly converted a rival's coin. Within three weeks mints as far apart as Spain and Egypt were producing reasonable and often highly artistic likenesses of the current emperor.

Nero committed suicide in June 68. Galba was proclaimed by troops in Spain and arrived in Rome in September. Coins were struck for him in Egypt in July and August (Year 1), though they seem to be more cartoon than likeness (Fig. 107). Galba was murdered in January 69 on the orders of Otho. Coins rushed out in February and March in Egypt show quite clearly Otho's Neronian-style toupee (Fig. 108).

107. Galba, (L–R) Egyptian *tetradrachmon*, July–August AD 68 (LA), struck by Tiberius Alexander, Prefect of Alexandria; *as* and *sestertius* struck after his occupation of Rome, September, AD 68 (£10, 1978; £1, 1978; £300, 1982 respectively).

108. Otho, (L–R) Egyptian *tetradrachmon*, January–April AD 69 (LA), struck by Tiberius Alexander; *denarius*, Rome, AD 69; *tetradrachmon*, Antioch, AD 69. Otho in fact never wore the wreath, withheld from him by the delaying tactics of the Senate, as was the right to strike bronze **SC** coin (£13, 1981; £380, 1981; £240, 1981 respectively).

After only ninety-five days Otho committed suicide in northern Italy and Vitellius advanced from Germany, reaching Rome in July. Coins preceded him and were also struck in Egypt. The same month, Vespasian was also proclaimed emperor and the Egyptian mint again sent out good likenesses of the fourth Emperor. The case for an official model portrait being a priority despatch is strong.

The development of portraits makes a fascinating study for the collector. Domitian's portrait as Caesar under his father and brother is wisp-bearded and resembles an infantile Mr Punch. It does show some basic similarity to the rugged chubbiness of Vespasian and Titus. Once Emperor, the rest of the Flavian family safely dead, his uninhibited megalomania demanded a different portrait. By AD 83 it is cast in the heroic style, clean-shaven, aquiline and firm (Fig. 109). It matches the victory messages of the reverses. In fact it is said to change more drastically than that of any other Emperor, even 'Caracalla'. The earlier portrait is probably the more true to life.

Domitian's successors seem to have slithered into their portraits by sloughing off those of their predecessors. Trajan assumed the purple early in AD 98, just after – possibly just before – Nerva's death. His first issue *sestertius* shows a distinctly Nerva-esque face, quite different

109. The faces of Domitian, (L–R) in AD 77; in AD 88; in AD 95.

from the Trajan commonly seen (Fig. 110). The coin even displays Nerva's titles while omitting **P(ater) P(atriae)**, as if covering some sort of interregnum. I discovered this coin in a general collector shop. The proprietor was as puzzled by it as I was intrigued. Trajan's coins are fairly common but this lingering portrait of a predecessor is in a class of its own.

In a similar fashion, the first issue *sestertius* of Hadrian follows the outlines of the bust of Trajan rather than the familiarly accepted one of Hadrian himself. Trajan's conquest titles form the legend but they are not seen again on Hadrian's bronze after the first issues. Either this was to acclimatise the population to a new emperor and lend legitimacy to the change in symbolic form, or more simply it may reveal the remodelling of older dies. Was there some delay in producing the official portrait? Was the die-cutter so used to doing the previous portrait that his hand followed certain key lines from sheer force of habit – until new blood and a fresh pair of eyes came to the Emperor's model profile on the graving table?

110. Nerva evolves into Trajan, (a) Nerva, AD 96. (b) Nerva, AD 97. (c) Trajan, January AD 98, the month of Nerva's death. (d) Trajan, c. AD 115.

PART II

THE ROMAN PROVINCIAL COINS

INTRODUCTION

Most collectors have seen the vast numbers of former British Empire
coins scattered around Britain. They carry the monarch's head and
titles, often resembling the island's own domestic coinage, yet ranging
from *piastres* and *rupees* down to the ubiquitous *cent*. Coins of Canada
and Australia still carry the current British monarch's head. The range
is so vast that to follow all the themes contained in British Imperial
local coinage in the widest sense would tax even the most skilful numismatic 'engineer'.

The Romans also had a vast quasi-independent provincial coinage
during the high centuries of the Empire. On the whole they represented
an amalgam of ancient local traditions and an aping of current
Imperial patterns. Sometimes they are crude, sometimes they are highly
artistic in their own right. They are frequently found in dealers' trays,
fairly worn, particularly those of bronze. In the great currency reforms
of AD 294–96, Diocletian rationalised the surviving provincial local
mints into branches of one great Imperial minting 'corporation', each
branch with its own distinctive mark and all following standards and
criteria for minting laid down by central government.

The situation is made more confusing when collectors discover that
prior to AD 294 not only did mints in the provinces strike coin for local
use based roughly on one or other Imperial tariff, but that local mints
also produced Imperial coin on occasion for general use. Britain's own
Royal Mint has also been known to subcontract the striking of sovereigns and of pennies in the recent past.

No satisfactory thumbnail sketch can be made of the vast flood of
local coinage under the Romans – summarising such a topic is like
trying to carry coal in thimbles. The collector might encounter coins
of Cappadocian Caesarea, Ephesus, Corinth or Alexandria, the latter
exclusively domestic yet still oddly tariffed against the Imperial *denarius*. Alexandria and Antioch (Athens was now somewhat over-
shadowed, rather like Winchester, a former capital of England) ranked
next to Rome in importance as the former capitals of great Empires
and, like most eastern cities, issued coinage which was in part a sop
to their faded glory. The Palestinian Jews had always been a special
case, a thorn in the flesh of any occupying power; they too were

respected, up to a point, in matters of the currency they were expected to handle. There were also the *coloniae* and the *castra*, now our Colognes, Lincolns, Chesters and Caerleons, settlements of former soldiers in strategic spots. A number of these had rights to coin, as for instance the naval settlement at *Nemausus* in Gaul, or *Flavia Neapolis* in Samaria (Fig. 111 see also Fig. 12).

Besides the sheer range of material, further hurdles face the collector of provincial coins: until recently there was no conveniently sized hand-book on the subject – mention has been made in Ch. IV of Sear's expensive new 'fist in the dyke', *Greek Imperial Coins and Their Values* (1982). Besides this, the puzzled collector has little else save the tens of volumes of the *British Museum Catalogue of Greek Imperial Coinage*. On top of tracts of scholarship (and acres of sites) still to be ploughed and reaped, the problems of language may deter and bewilder those who are just managing to cope with basic Latin legends. Some coins are inscribed in Hebrew, some in Greek (and adulterated Greek) and some in a mixture of Latin and Greek, frequently abbreviated to add to the confusion.

Despite all this apparent discouragement, local coins from the Roman provinces have much to recommend them to the collector. They are a mine of large and medium bronzes, sometimes at relatively low cost, although many tend to be worn. There is even good reason for the wear. While inflation drove out large bronze in the west due to the increase of debased and token silver, eastern bronzes became more and more a metal-content-value currency because of the relative absence of silver.

Provincials also offer portraits which might be otherwise impossible or too expensive to obtain in rare Imperial issues – Otho, Antinoüs and Poppaea are cases in point. Countermarks, ranging from abbre-viated legends to busts, goddesses and regimental titles provide 'coins within coins' for the collector, even though scholars are often unable to interpret them. In short, despite (or because of?) occasional crudity, general wear and overall incomprehensibility, Roman provincial issues are the source of many a collector's bargain.

While the coinage of Alexandria and Palestine gives some idea of local minting in the more peaceful and the more disturbed provinces, the coins of Roman Britain were not of course the products of a semi-independent authority. However, due to ingenious local devices for meeting shortage of coin in the province, as well as the occasional use of the island as an offshore base for proclaiming an adventurer's inde-pendence, Roman coins from Britain have their own characteristics, often peculiar to the province alone. Rome's desperate need for silver and copper sources for her currency was, after all, one of the main reasons for occupying the land of the *gentes barbaras trans Oceanum* (Clad-dius' Arch, see Fig. 3).

111. (a) *As* of *Nemausus* (Nîmes) struck under Augustus before 10 BC. The heads of the two commanders reminded the naval veterans of this Gallic *colonia* of their moment of glory at Actium. The Egyptian crocodile is shown tethered to a palm-tree. (b) *Ae 27 mm* of Tyre, Syro Phoenicia, with the vexillum of *colonia* of **Legion III** *Gallica*, part of the Syrian garrison under Severus. (c) *Ae 38 mm*, Geta and Caracalla, Ephesus. Both brother Emperors on horseback before the statue of Artemis. Once a great city of Asia Minor, famous for its Temple of Artemis, Ephesus prospered again under Roman rule. (d) *Ae 33 mm*, Gordian III, Synnada, Phrygia, Asia Minor. Emperor in chariot. A major city of an ancient Greek kingdom, it once boasted Midas as its king.

VII

JUDEA IN PALESTINE – A PRICKLY PROVINCE

112.

(This monument called) **TIBERIEUM**
(Its builder, Po) **NTIUS PILATUS**
(Dedicated while Prae) **FECTUS IUDAEAE.**

Inscription found at Caesarea, 1961,
first archeological evidence of Pilatus'
name and rank

Palestine was one of Rome's buffer states in the east. A single kingdom
under the half-Jewish king and client-king of Augustus, Herod the

Great, it was divided between his sons on his death in 4 BC. Archelaus proved unfit to govern the southern part of the territory and in AD 6 Roman prefects took over the direct rule of Judea and Samaria until AD 41.

The Gospel coins

To an experienced collector the world's best known first-century books, the Gospels, can also read like the world's first handbook on ancient coins! This may not be purely accidental detail. Matthew, traditionally placed somewhere in the production process of the longest of the Gospels, seems to have spent his early life as a finance officer on the staff of Prince Herod Antipas in Galilee.

The subject is much written about and often incorrectly. This is not surprising considering that there were seven different strands of currency in circulation together, all cross-tariffed and some of them already showing a century of wear by the time of Jesus. Roman jingled along with Seleucid, Ptolomaic, Herodian, Antiochean, Tyrian and so-called 'Procuratorial'. With good reason Matthew refers to the wise spirituality of a man who is like a financier knowing how to combine together in his transactions 'new and old (coins) out of the same cash box'.

The English word *penny* has been used to translate both *denarius* and *as* as well as the *quadrans*. Judas' bloodmoney, simply *argurion* (or its Constantinian equivalent in Jerome's translation, *argenteus*) according to Matthew, has been variously rendered as *denarius* and *tetradrachmon*. Since the latter was four times the value of the former it makes a difference to our understanding of the pressures on the man.

Matthew the financier mentions the *stater, denarius, didrachmon, as*(*sarion*), *quadrans* and *chalkos*. The other Gospels add the *lepton* and *drachma* as well as the reckoning multiples of *mina* and *talanton* (talent). The reason for the complexity is obvious. Palestine was continually under some foreign occupier, whether Greek, Syrian, Persian, Roman or Rome's puppet prince. Jesus, for instance, was born under the client King Herod about 6 BC. He grew up in Galilee under the client-prince Herod Antipas and died in Jerusalem, the territory of the Roman Prefect of Judea and Samaria. Small wonder that at one stage he had to ask questions about the silver *denarius* of the tax. If the cross-matched currency of the area puzzled those who used it, the bewildered collector should take heart.

The bronze *lepton* (in Hebrew, *prutah*, smallest copper, possibly derived from a slang name, 'grape-pip',) was the smallest coin valued at around eight to a copper *as*. Roman prefects who took over the Herodian mint in AD 6 inherited and exercised to the full the Herodian privilege as well as the prefect's traditional right to strike coin in small bronze. This 'mite' (*lepton* literally means 'trivial thing') was the back-bone of currency among a poor population. By itself it could buy a pomegranate or a lemon. Eight could buy sparrows from the cheap end of the butcher's counter. A woman, so the proverb ran, could just about be trusted with one. When Jesus spotted a widow giving two *lepta* to the Temple, he commented on her generosity. Her coins could have been older Herodian currency, but it is more likely they were the new ones struck by the Romans in volume. Between AD 6 and AD 31, four out of five prefects struck coin. Coponius, Ambibulus and Gratus kept traditional Jewish types and seem to have been respected by the Jews (Fig. 113a and b). Coponius even had a Temple gate named after him, unique for a Gentile. Pilatus, the fifth governor, seems to have been less tactful, placing Imperial religious symbols on his issues (Fig. 113c, see also Fig. 118). We know that he committed many gaffes against the

113. Prefects' *lepta*, or *Ae 15 mm*: (a) Ambibulus, AD 9–12, (b) Gratus, AD 15–26. After Ambibulus who dated his coins from Actium, 31 BC, coins were dated from the start of the current reign (£0.50, 1970 and £20, 1979, respectively). (c) Pontius Pilatus, AD 26–36, with barley ears and a *simpulum* (see Fig. 118) one of two *lepta* thought to have left marks on the Turin Shroud. (From the ruins of Sebaste, Samaria.)

Jews before Tiberius dismissed him in AD 36. Possibly he had to deal with a more assertive and restless generation than Coponius and that for a whole decade, longer than most other Roman administrators of the area.

Did the images on the coins really cause religious offence? Was there that much to choose between the emperor's head and the head of Melkart on Tyrian silver? Perhaps the offence was traditional rather than actively felt. The inscription on the Roman *denarii* which called the emperor 'High Priest' and his predecessor 'Divine' was certainly against all that the Jewish religion held dear. Roman Imperial coins were in fact banned from religious use, but if the principle had been a strictly and widely applied rule the finances of Palestine would have been paralysed. Besides, Tyrian silver had an universally accepted standard of fineness.

Jesus warned his disciples to work in poverty, 'taking neither gold nor silver nor *chalkoi*'. Matthew's Greek word could cover either a *lepton* or more likely a *semis*-sized bronze (see Fig. 93). The debtor, notes Matthew, cannot leave prison until he has paid up the last *quadrans*. Luke changes this to a *lepton* and perhaps Matthew's Galilean work explains why he totally ignores the smallest Judean coin.

Although there is little hint of inflation in the Gospels, the bulk-buying mentality is evident. Matthew notes that the copper *as(sarion)* could buy two sparrows for protein soup, but Luke with the housewife in mind (his is sometimes called 'the Gospel for women') noted that five such birds could be bought for two *asses*.

The *sestertius* makes no appearance at all but there was plenty of silver variety to make up for it. *Drachmai* from Cappadocian Caesarea, *tetradrachma* from Tyre and Antioch, *denarii* from Rome were all roughly tariffed against each other, using the *denarius* as the basic unit. No doubt the margin of error in the approximation was in favour of the money-changer.

A *denarius* was the vineyard-worker's daily pay. The Samaritan in the parable handed over two *denarii* to the innkeeper for the mugging victim. A prostitute poured perfume worth 300 *denarii* over Jesus' head and feet. Two debtors in the parable of forgiveness owed very different sums – 500 and 50 *denarii* respectively. A similar parable in Matthew has a debtor let off the fantastic amount of 10,000 *talanta* (60 million *denarii*!); he then proceeds to throttle a man who owed him a mere 100 *denarii*.

Direct tax went to Rome in the form of the *denarius* and possibly the newly arrived Cappadocian *drachma*, both with a guaranteed silver content. Both carried Latin inscriptions (the Cappadocian coins changed to Greek under the Flavians) and were not easily distinguished at first sight. Roman officers, no doubt suitably protected, collected this tribute. Then as now, tax was disliked. To trap Jesus, some of his religious leaders asked his opinion of Roman taxation – should it be paid at all?

114. *Denarii*, Tiberius, AD 14–37, traditionally regarded as the tax coin or 'tribute penny' of the Gospel incident. Livia is seated as Pax (£35, 1978 and £90, 1981). (See also Fig. 52.)

Whatever the answer, he would have had to make a political judgement either for Rome or for the nationalists. He asked for a coin of the tax (Fig. 114). Had this artisan little experience of silver? How often did a Galilean see a Roman *denarius*? When Jesus asked 'whose image and inscription' was on the *denarius* was this because he could not read Latin or because the busts of Augustus and Tiberius were barely distinguishable to the easterner? The only recorded answer was 'Caesar's', but among collectors Tiberius is the favourite, partly because he was the emperor of the day, partly because his coinage is so much simpler than the vast variety of Augustus' silver. (There would also have been older *denarii* in circulation from previous brief encounters with the Rome of Pompey and of Mark Antony.)

However offensive the Roman coin might have been for religious reasons there seemed to be no scruple about keeping it in the wallet. Jesus finally replied that if the silver was Caesar's in the first place then they owed him for the privilege of using it. It should not be elevated into a mock religious issue just to serve some partisan viewpoint.

Luke has a strange story of a woman who loses one of ten *drachmai*. She sweeps the house frantically, finds it and then celebrates with friends. Why such fuss? This parable of God's love makes no sense until it is realised that a married woman wore her dowry or widow's pension sewn onto her best headdress. Occasionally the threaded coins broke loose, possibly in washing. Ten *drachmai* was a poor enough portion and to lose one tenth of this was a crisis. To illustrate this I have chosen a tiny *hemidrachma* from Cappadocia where a large Christian community already flourished in Luke's time (Fig. 115). It too is pierced for wear.

Tyre and Antioch supplied higher denominations of silver. Every Jew paid tax in the early spring to the Temple funds. Jesus was

115. *Hemidrachma*, Nero, Caesarea in Cappadocia, *c.* AD 59, pierced and plugged (£6, 1978).

approached and asked for the two-*drachma* levy by the Temple agents. Peter paid out a *stater* on behalf of them both from the proceeds of his trawling. Some English translations call this a *shekel* but Matthew does not use this word. It had ultra-nationalist overtones. The *shekel* appeared briefly in the Jewish Revolt of AD 66–70 and again in 1980 under the Israeli government currency reforms. After the Temple fell in AD 70 the *didrachmon* or two-*denarii* tax was still taken from all Jews, this time to subsidise the worship of Jupiter in Rome. A rare *sestertius* of Nerva marks when that lawyer-emperor cleared up the scandalous way in which this money was being squeezed from anyone thought to be even remotely Jewish (see Fig. 15a).

Stater was in fact the colloquial Greek name applied in this case to the Tyrian *tetradrachmon* (Fig. 116). The coin was less offensive than Roman silver and was used in religious affairs. Since Judas was paid the legal price of a slave's life from Temple coffers this must have been the coin he received. Matthew simply calls them 'thirty silvers' but with his eye for finance is the only Gospel writer to detail the amount.

Matthew in fact introduces far more coins more frequently than any other Gospel writer. He mentions taxmen more frequently; he alone mentions the Temple tax and the gold at Christ's birth; today he might have been a metal-detector enthusiast since he also is the only one to speak of the man who sold everything to buy a field in which treasure was buried! It appears that he worked for Antipas at Capernaum on the Galilee lake as a collector of customs dues. He draws on his experience of forgeries and of the range of coinage in circulation. The local trawlermen had little reason to like him or his kind. His master's new capital at Tiberias just down the lake-shore earns no mention in the Gospels. Not surprisingly, his medieval symbol was the moneybag. Appropriately enough for the world's best known coin enthusiast, he was regarded as the patron saint of bankers and financiers.

116. *Tetradrachmon* of Tyre, 115 BC, Melkart, the sea-god patron of the port (£350, 1981).

For today's budget collector interested in this theme, the *lepton* can still be found for a few pounds and even less if discovered unrecognised in rummage trays. It tends to be badly struck and is usually worn. While some ancient silver is very highly priced, as for instance the Tyrian *tetradrachmon* (a reproduction fills the gap in my collection), the so-called 'tribute penny' of Tiberius is not uncommon and can still be bought for two figures – and for less if plated.

The Shroud of Turin and the collector

The much publicized Shroud of Turin is a four-metre strip of linen which has been housed for more than four centuries in the cathedral of that city. It bears the authentic but so far inexplicable imprint of

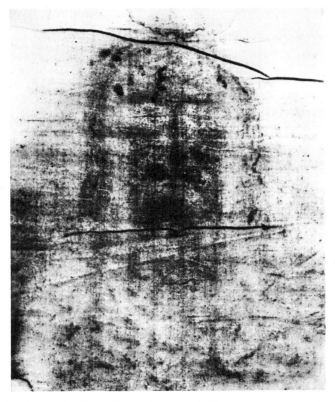

117. The face of the Turin Shroud – *lepta* of Pilatus are now thought to have covered the eyes of the corpse. The mark on the bruised eye is clearer than on the other and is thought to be the mark of a *lituus lepton*.

the front and back of a man's body. Traces of injuries to the body have led to a general belief that it is the burial cloth draped over the body of Christ after the crucifixion. (The Gospels do note that linen as well as a tomb was provided by the wealthy Joseph of Arimathea.) In recent years it has undergone the most stringent scientific analysis at the hands of the USAF (NASA), Kodak and several universities.

In 1977 USAF scientists, using an image analyser from their space programme, announced the possibility of coin traces over the eyes of the imprinted figure. Their dimensional analysis showed that there had been unusual protuberances over the eyes. Further study suggested the marks were coin-shaped, less than 20 mm in diameter (Fig. 117). Covering dead eyes was an ancient and widespread practice. It meets the human need to be spared the stare of the dead and was seen as a traditional payment to the ferryman who guided the dead into the great unknown. The Jews gave the custom a fresh interpretation: eyes which had seen God at the moment of death ought not to be defiled by staring at mere creation afterwards.

In 1980 came a claim from Chicago's Loyola University that one of the 'coin' traces shows the imprint of a crook staff. The claim was confirmed in 1981 and 1982 by computer analysis in independent US universities, although this still has to meet the scrutiny of other scholars and experts. The crook was once part of the Roman Emperor's regalia as high priest and occurs as a tiny detail on a number of Imperial coins (Fig. 118a). It was used as a focusing frame when reading the signs of the stars. On only one known coin is the device a dominant type – a *lepton* of Pontius Pilatus struck in two issues around AD 30–31 (Fig. 118b). Pilatus issued three dates of coin; two carried the crook staff, one carried the divination ladle used by the Emperor in animal sacrifices. Both were tactless attempts to honour Tiberius and jar Jewish sensibilities.

The crook staff issues are not renowned for their quality – perhaps control was lax at the Caesarea mint during Pilatus' time. Poor strikings with poor dies show a decline after the earlier Prefects' bronzes.

118. (a) The ritual instruments of the Emperor as Pontifex Maximus, including the *lituus* (crook) and the *simpulum* (dipper-ladle), both of which feature on Pilatus' coins. (b) *Lepton* of Pilatus showing *lituus* and the word **TIBERIOS** struck *c.* AD 31. (£15, 1978, Museum disposal).

Possibly Jewish die-cutters, usually less than happy anyway working in Greek, were also conducting their own mild form of industrial sabotage against Pilatus' irksome rule. The current price of between £15 and £30 for a Pilatus *lepton* would astound the widow at the Temple collection box no less than the Caesarea mint-worker.

The *lepton* was the only remotely distinctive Jewish coin left, a concession to a proud race under Roman rule. If placed on the eyes of a corpse it can only have been a gesture – 15 mm covers only a corner of the eye socket. Confirmation of this finding would at least date and locate the first use of the Shroud even if it could not allow identification of the corpse it covered. It might also give an interesting slant on an old Jewish saying which claimed that the Messiah would not come until the last of the tens of thousands of tiny *lepta* disappeared – that is, a long time to come.

The Shroud itself seems to have travelled much between its eastern origin and Turin. One theory, based on ancient traditions and now apparently confirmed by analysis of pollen grains caught in its fibres, is that it was kept at Edessa in Syria, the world's first Christian state, and hidden in a wall until the late sixth century. It may then have been on display for over 300 years, but folded, showing only the face – hence the legends of the 'Veron-ica' towel.

From the collector's angle, it is interesting that art historians link the conventional long-haired, bearded full-face Christ to shortly after the Shroud's sixth-century reappearance. This Christ figure again begins to dominate later Byzantine coins around the time the Edessa 'towel' was taken to Constantinople (Fig. 119a). Copper versions of the same icon, unattractive and usually badly worn, can be found for pence in rummage trays (Fig. 119b). The traditional Christ of the Byzantine mosaics shows all the features of the Shroud figure from that date, including a kiss-curl dropping over the forehead. On the cloth it is in fact a bloodstain curling down from the hairline. The eyes of the icon also protrude.

a

b

119. (a) Gold *solidus*, Constantinople, Constantius VII and Romanus II, AD 945, the year after the 'towel' of Edessa was brought to Constantinople. (b) Common, worn Byzantine *follis* of the same era, frequently found in dealers rummage trays.

The First Jewish Revolt, AD 66–70

The rebel Jewish *shekel* and the Roman palm tree *sestertius* are standard book illustrations. Understandably they are sought after by connoisseurs and at today's three and four figure prices they are forbidden fruit to most collectors. Sheer recognition of any Jewish coins can be a further obstacle to adopting this theme, however interesting. (Herod) Agrippa I died in AD 44 (Fig. 120). A further succession of Roman governors, now procurators, ruled up to AD 66, ostensibly allowing (Marcus) Agrippa II to come of age to take the throne of Judea. Only Procurator Felix (AD 52–60) struck coins (Fig. 121). Despite marrying Marcus' sister, his harsh and corrupt administration was a root cause of Jewish unrest. Evidently obsessed with money, he even tried to extort it from his famous prisoner, Paul of Tarsus. His second issue of coin in AD 58 was larger than those of the previous ten governors put together. Money was in the blood: his brother had been Claudius' finance minister.

Three governors later, in AD 66, revolt flared up in Jerusalem. Procurator Gessius Florus had been the last straw. His holding force in the city was attacked and the Legate of Syria moved south with more

120. *Lepton*, (Herod) Agrippa I, King of Palestine AD 37/41–4, struck in AD 42. This volume striking is still relatively commonly encountered in rummage trays as far apart as Israel and England. We have turned the regal sunshade of the East into a portable rain shelter for the North! (£1, 1982).

121. *Lepton*, Procurator Felix AD 52–60, struck AD 58 in great volume – a feature of Nero's reign throughout the Empire. **NERONOS** appears inside the laurel wreath; a palm accompanies the date (£1, 1982).

troops, only to be driven off. Nero had been competing in the Olympic Games, strumming for prizes while the Empire smouldered around him. He handed over the task of subduing Palestine to Vespasian, a soldier blooded in Germany and in the invasion of Britain (Fig. 122). Starting in the north with 60,000 troops, Vespasian rolled up the little country like a carpet strip. Galilee and Samaria were largely put to the sword. The Jewish commander in Galilee gave himself up and survived into old age in Rome under the telling name of Josephus *Flavius*. There he wrote our chief, if partisan, account of the war.

By the spring of AD 68 the revolt was contained into the Jerusalem area. The nearby hills, desert and coast came under Vespasian's control. Qumran on the Dead Sea seems to have been destroyed at this date, but not before hiding its library in nearby caves. The manuscripts discovered in 1947 by an Arab boy idly throwing stones became known to the excited public as 'the Dead Sea Scrolls'.

Inside Jerusalem the rebel government began striking silver coin early in AD 67, dating them **shekel of Year One** and **of Year Two** of the new, independent **Zion**. The Greek denominational names of *stater* and *tetradrachmon* had no place in revolt currency. The coin, with its chalice and pomegranates, is famous but out of the range of most collectors' purses (Fig. 123).

Much more commonly obtainable are the numerous *prutot* of **Year Two** (AD 67–8), with chalice and vineleaf and the inscription **The**

122. Vespasian and Titus, father and son, successive commanders in the Jewish war and successive Emperors afterwards. *Sestertii.*

123. *Sheklim*, Jewish Revolt, Years One, Two and Three. The date features above the chalice of salvation and the denomination **Shekel Israel** surrounds it; the reverse shows three pomegranates (often called a triple lily!) with the legend **Jerusalem the Holy**. (Estimate at auction, 1982, up to £800 each.)

Freedom of Zion. Many were overstruck onto procurators' *lepta* (Fig. 124a). Made in great numbers in the exuberance of **Year Two** (Year One saw no bronze), they were cast away after the revolt as worthless, possibly even dangerous. The 'grape pip' met a grape pip's end. Little used, their condition is often quite good (Fig. 124b).

Nero's suicide in June AD 68 signalled a half-time break in the Jewish war. Vespasian did not press the siege of Jerusalem but hung fire until in July AD 69 he himself was declared emperor and left for Rome. His son Titus then continued the campaign. As Chief-of-Staff with useful local knowledge he had Tiberius Alexander, Jewish Prefect of Egypt and a former procurator of Judea.

Blockaded by four legions, rebel morale dropped. The coinage thinned – silver was scarce. Much had been used on *sheklim* of previous years. Refugees had fled with it and none could be imported. *Sheklim* of **Year Five** are the rarest. After the siege the silver was worth looting or recycling, hence the present scarcity of *sheklim* in contrast to the bronze. Some bronze *sheklim* exist – emergency money for later redemp-

124. *Prutot*, Jewish Revolt, Year Two (AD 67–8). The two-handled water jar of the Temple hints at a free religion while the vineleaf and the inscription **Freedom of Sion !** proclaim national independence in a country sometimes called 'God's vineyard'. Such coins are usually crude rather than worn since the period of circulation was brief; they were last used by the defenders of Masada for ration tokens, as late as AD 72. (a) The uneven design below the chalice and internal eccentric circumferences at 8 o'clock, mark an overstrike on a Procurator's coin. (b) Obverse and reverse of another example (£1–8, depending on the dealer!).

tion. The bronze *prutot* of **Year Four** also change their tune to reflect the times. They now proclaim **The Redemption of Zion**, a prayer rather than the war cry of Year Two. (See Fig. 85).

The city fell district by district. In the heat of battle the Romans set fire to the Sanctuary in the Temple area. The white gilded complex had just been completed after eighty years of building. Now it was a fortress, an ancient Monte Cassino. Today, only its vast platform survives. The strict Jew will go onto the site only as far as the foot of the western supporting wall, the 'Wailing Wall'. The site has been defiled and the Boar pennant of Legion X *Fretensis* (see Fig. 12) desecrated the 'Holy of Holies'. By September AD 70 Jerusalem was sacked and largely gutted by fire. To the Jews and early Christians it was like the end of the world, literally the apocalypse now.

Rome celebrated in grisly manner. Prisoners were crucified, drowned in the Dead Sea, used as gladiator bait or turned into navvies for the new Corinthian Canal. Fugitives were chased into nearby Egypt and over 100,000 went to slave labour in Rome where they built the Flavian amphitheatre (Colosseum) and the Arch of Titus. The Temple treasures also went to Rome and were kept there on display until they disappeared from record around AD 190.

To mark the victory, Vespasian and Titus struck the **Iudaea Capta** series of coins between AD 71 and 80. These coins, particularly the *sestertii*, command quite high prices. They can, however, be found in lower grades of condition (Fig. 125). After all, vast quantities were struck, the largest Roman commemoration in coin of a single event. They came, with variations, from Palestine itself, where (Marcus) Agrippa II struck in Greek, as well as from mints in Spain, Gaul, Italy and Cappadocia. It was an important victory. Palestine was the stage for Vespasian's accession. The Empire needed his military rule after Nero and the anarchy of AD 68–9. Outsiders beyond the frontier needed warning that Rome could assert herself. There were more reasons for the extravagance of coin than mere relief at crushing a revolt or simple anti-semitism.

The first coins were already showing two years wear before the final curtain came down on the Jewish war. A number of rebels had withdrawn to the desert in AD 66. They moved onto Masada, the deserted mountain palace built a century before by Herod the Great. Although mopping-up operations began in AD 71, Masada was invested last of all. The rebels held out there until April AD 73, when nearly 1,000 committed suicide rather than allow themselves to be taken.

The Bar 'Kochba' Revolt, AD 132–35

'Year Zero' of the Jewish people in AD 70 did not spell the end of Jewish religion or culture in Palestine. The embers of aspirations to inde-

125. Worn Roman commemorative coins of the Judean victory: (a) *As*, Titus as Caesar, Lyons, AD 77, female Judea under palm (£18, 1979). (b) *Sestertius*, Vespasian, AD 71, prisoners and arms under palm; **Iudaea Capta !** legend almost obliterated. Twenty-five different variants of this design were struck at four western mints. (£25, 1979). (c) *Sestertius*, Vespasian, AD 71, Spain; Victory attaches shield to palm tree; the legend **Victoria Augusti !** is almost obliterated. (d) *Denarius*, Titus, June 79, with kneeling male prisoner and trophy of the Judean campaign (£4, 1970).

pendence flickered for a moment in the reign of Trajan and then seemed to die away. At the peak of Hadrian's reign in AD 132 a second violent and initially successful revolt flared up, now known by the Aramaic name of its leader.

Hadrian had visited Jerusalem, or what was left of it, in AD 130. His plans for the thoroughly Roman rebuilding of the city may have sparked off the revolt – we simply do not know. Sources for this war are scrappy and sometimes conflicting, based on the partisan jottings of rabbis, hostile Christian historians, coins and, since their discovery in 1951 in a cave, a bundle of letters signed by Bar 'Kochba' himself. At least from these we know that he signed himself (sometimes in Hebrew, sometimes in Aramaic dialect – he used both) **Simeon ben/bar Koseba** (son of Koseba). His followers, looking for the expected Messiah, saw in his name the star (**Kochba**) which would herald the leader. Playing the same word-game, anti-Jewish Christians in resentment against

Simeon's treatment of their number called him **bar 'Koziba'** (son of a lie). Understandably Simeon has taken on some of the aura of a Palestinian Arthur.

He was strategist enough to carve out from Roman rule in AD 132 a territory the size of Judea. The massacre of Legion XXII *Deiotariana* and the capture of the baggage trains gave him access to Imperial silver (Fig. 126). He held Jerusalem. At some mint in the vicinity of the city he struck silver and bronze in his own name and with distinctly Hebrew types. Sensibly he appropriated and overstruck *denarii, tetradrachma*, and *asses* from Antioch. His mintmasters seem to have made few blank flans. The Temple, now only a memory some sixty years old, features on the largest silver overstrikes. On the others, palm trees and vine leaves take the place of the Imperial bust and motifs (Fig. 127). He styled himself Prince of Israel – presumably God alone was King. Collectors can pick up his bronzes, often in good condition, at low two-figure prices.

This successful guerrilla war lost its initial momentum and like the first revolt was defeated by sheer weight of Roman numbers. Hadrian himself came into the campaign – the Legate of Britain came 3,000 miles to his assistance. In AD 135 a determined effort subdued many strong-points and made away with a suggested 0.5 million lives. The revolt – and Simeon – ended in a last stand to the south of Jerusalem under the relentless sun of a Judean summer. 'From that time' noted Eusebius with some glee, 'the entire race has been forbidden to set foot anywhere in the neighbourhood of Jerusalem. (The city) was colonised by an alien race (and) changed its name (to Aelia) in honour of Aelius Hadrianus.' (Fig. 128a).

Astrology and the signs of the heavens were important to all cultures

126. ex-*Denarius*, requisitioned and overstruck by Bar 'Kochba' as a ready made flan for a quarter-shekel. *Obv*: the name **Shimon** in wreath, some traces of Latin lettering visible at 4 o'clock. *Rev*: jug and palm branch, Hebrew inscription **Freedom of Israel** (partially lost due to flatstriking). If the coin is turned through 180° the legend **Aug PM Co** can be seen clearly surmounting the head of (?) Vespasian, his profile extending from the right hand side of the inverted jar. The fineness of a Roman *denarius* of this period would not match that ritually required for a *shekel* (£300 upwards, 1982).

127. Bronze coins of Bar 'Kochba': (a) *Ae 25 mm, c.* AD 134, struck near Jerusalem; palm tree and dates shelter the name **Shimon** and a vineleaf is surrounded by the slogan **Freedom of Jerusalem!** (£15. 1979). (b) Smaller bronze with lyre and palm branch (from £20 to £100, 1982, depending on condition).

of the ancient world. Hadrian issued moonsilver *denarii* with the crescent and a fixed number of stars to announce a new age and a world ruler (Fig. 128c). Bar 'Kochba' and for that matter any messiah fulfilling the prophecy of the star of Jacob and David would literally be seen as a rival 'superstar' and by definition intolerable.

128. (a) *Sestertius*, Hadrian, commemorating his visit to the Syrian garrison just prior to the Bar 'Kochba' revolt; this garrison took the brunt of the early fighting until support came from other parts of the Empire. Julius Severus, seconded governor of Britain, finally cornered and defeated the rebel forces in AD 135 (estimated at *c.* £300, 1980). (b) *Sestertius*, Hadrian, *c.* AD 136, the Emperor being welcomed back by the helmeted figure of Roma. Although it is a general commemoration of his travels, unintentionally it also marks his last great return to Rome, after the Bar 'Kochba' rebellion had been put down (see Fig. 59). (c) *Denarius*, Hadrian, pierced with rivet still in place at 12 o'clock. The moon and seven stars made an ideal amulet – the even more worn obverse and the position of the rivet are indications that it was worn reverse outwards (£1, rummage tray, 1980).

VIII

EGYPT AND BRITAIN – PROVINCES APART

> Not even the fearsome tribesmen of Britain or Germany
> or the fighting Poles or the hulking Romanians ever went
> so berserk as this useless unwarlike rabble, who rig scraps
> of sail on their earthenware feluccas and row with diminu-
> tive oars in painted crockery skiffs.
>
> Juvenal, *Satire* XV, *c.* AD 130

Aegyptus

129. *Ae 35 mm, drachma,* Hadrian, *c.* AD 129, the Nile reclining on a crocodile.
The date appears in letters in the exergue, **Twelve**. (£13, 1982. Irreverently
dubbed by collectors, 'manhole covers'!).

Juvenal had no time for the Egyptians, it is obvious. Many collectors
of Roman coin have little idea of, or no time at all for the crudely struck
coins of this North African province. In fact, the Romans themselves
forbade that provincial money leave Egypt or that Imperial money be
taken there. Even senators were forbidden to go there. In the complex
world of provincial coinage, that of Roman Egypt was probably the
simplest, most self-contained and the nearest the Romans ever came
to our own token paper money.

Egypt was the emperor's private property, a trophy of war after Actium in 31 BC and the subsequent deaths of Mark Antony and Cleopatra. With her the Ptolemies ended. Octavian took over the Egyptian crown as well as the laurels of Rome. The grain for which Egypt was so prized was exported to Rome – in tribute, not as commerce. The deserts were a useful sink to which exiles could be relegated under supervision. This may have happened to Juvenal himself under Domitian, hence his hostility. Augustus kept Egypt well apart from the rest of provincial affairs. By the reign of Tiberius Rome had reverted to a local Egyptian coinage modelled on the last debased *tetradrachma* of the house of Ptolemy. They were notionally valued at one to the *denarius* (Fig. 130).

130. (a) *Ae 25 mm*, Cleopatra VII, 51–30 BC, last of the Ptolemaic rulers of Egypt. (b) *Tetradrachmon*, Alexandria, *c.* AD 21 (Year Seven), the first of the Roman Imperial coins of the province, struck by Tiberius and showing Augustus on the reverse (£250, 1981).

Scholars have concluded that the Egyptians themselves, let alone the Romans, had little use for their money outside the cosmopolitan population of urban Alexandria. The rural natives lived by barter but the needs of the second most important city in the Empire, with its population of over 0.5 million, were enough to justify a mint. Coinage was issued in some years but not in others. The mint is thought to have operated mainly in the summer months, to coincide with trade from the harvest in the hinterland. However, the coinage of Otho, for instance, who reigned only from January to April AD 69, suggests additional periods of volume production (see Fig. 108). Unskilled labour may well have been drafted in for peak outputs – the results seem evident in the standard of some coins. Under Nero, when production broke all records, the coins differ in weight – 7–14 gms and in diameters – 23–29 mms! (Fig. 131).

Egyptian coins are dated by the calendar symbol **L** followed by the alphabet-number of the year of the Emperor's reign (see Basic Greek terms on p. 175). Like school, the Egyptian calendar began at the end of August. This convenient and easily understood dating system holds an added attraction for modern collectors.

At first, the base silver Imperial *tetradrachma* were strictly 25 per cent fine. They seem to have been tariffed at one *denarius* rather than the

131. (a) *Tetradrachmon*, Nero, Year Twelve (AD 65) with Alexandria on the reverse (£10, 1979). (b) As above, but treble-struck, misshapen, and light-weight (7 gms) – evidence of unskilled labour or lax quality control in a year noted for its volume production (£3, 1978).

usual three or four for such a denomination. Possibly old *denarii* were mixed with exactly three times as much base metal in the individual moulds. Nero, who minted vast numbers of these coins after AD 64 just as he did in the west, likewise reduced the silver content to about 16 per cent. By the time of Domitian there were a further five denominations in bronze. These lasted until the early third century when the base or billon silver was so debased as to make bronze redundant. *Tetradrachma* quit the Egyptian scene in AD 296, reduced in size and with a silver content as low as 1 per cent. The portraits on these later coins are often good and usually clear while the bronze is much better than that of western inflation money of the same period (Fig. 132). From AD 294, when Diocletian rationalised the production of Imperial currency, Alexandria took her place (and her mark **ALE**) as a regular mint of the Empire (Fig. 133). Latin ousted the Greek of the Ptolemies and western minting techniques took the place of cruder eastern methods.

Egyptian coins are often found on domestic sites, 'banked' under the floor, sometimes in thousands. They are also preserved by the dry climate of the country. Troops digging during the desert campaigns of both World Wars frequently uncovered coins in good condition. The earlier base silver *tetradrachma* are also found in India where they might have been acceptable as trading currency, their silver content perhaps overrated. Some of the later bronze *tetradrachma* also appear in England, but their presence in Lancashire gardens is more to do with tours of duty by the Lancashire Fusiliers and a 48-hour pass into Cairo than with some unrecorded legion in Wigan. Beware the feverish imagination of the collector!

132. The last *tetradrachma* of Imperial Egypt: (a) Diocletian with Equity (*Dikaiosuné*), Year Two (AD 285). (b) Maximian with Spes (*Elpis*), Year Two (AD 287). The coins ended during these same reigns, AD 296/7.

133. The new mintmark **ALE(xandria)** on a *follis* of Diocletian, AD 305. Jupiter holds Victory. Struck in Section 4 of the mint (£65, 1981).

There are bargains for the picking. Nero's *tetradrachma* are often boldly struck, little worn and good value for their portraits. In a vast output he featured many reverse portraits as well, including Augustus, Tiberius and two of his wives (Fig. 134). Reverse portraits offer double value to a collector; there are no contemporary portraits of Augustus from Egypt, while those of Tiberius tend to be expensive because of their rarity and fineness. It is also advisable to look carefully at any female portrait on the Nero reverses since the common figure of Alexandria can easily be mistaken for the more valuable portrait of one of the wives.

134. *Tetradrachmon*, Nero, Year Thirteen (AD 66) with Augustus on the reverse struck by Tiberius Alexander, Prefect of Alexandria (£14, 1980).

Otho and Vitellius, whose coins might otherwise be too much for the collector's purse, can be acquired more easily in *tetradrachmon* form, crude but still portraits (see Fig. 108). Much more expensive is the coin commemorating Hadrian's male lover, Antinoüs, who threw himself into the Nile in AD 130 after some petty quarrel with the travelling Emperor (Fig. 135). Hadrian wept at his death and the coins reflected his feelings. It is still possible to find worn versions of these, overlooked and unidentified because of condition as well as origin.

The large bronzes of Trajan, Hadrian himself and Antoninus Pius with their hub-dents and their bevelled edges are easily recognised on the dealer's tray. Usually worn, they are easily dateable. They tend to be the *drachmai* and *hemidrachmai*, apparently modelled on the Imperial *sestertii* and *dupondii*. Their reverse designs occasionally boast highly unusual and original designs such as the Nilometer (flood-level gauge for the Nile) or the goddess Isis trapping the wind in a sail with the famous lighthouse in the background. A series of Antoninus Pius displays the signs of the zodiac (Fig. 136). For us, just as for the ancient colonised Egyptian, they are the 'poor man's *sestertii*' in an age where demand for the large artistic coin has taken many Imperial *sestertii* out of the market flow.

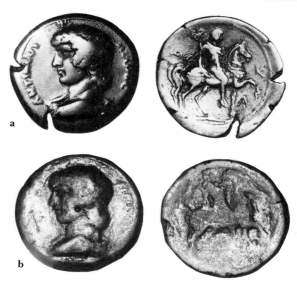

135. *Ae 35 mm, drachma,* posthumous of Antinoüs, Hadrian's homosexual lover. The youth features in portrait and astride a horse as Hermes. The worn coin, while considerably cheaper, was still expensive. ((a) Estimate at auction, £900, 1981, (b) sold for £95, 1980.)

136. *Ae 35 mm, drachmai,* Antoninus Pius, some of a series showing the Zodiac. (a) Venus in Tauris (£140, 1980). (b) Sun in Leo (£350, 1980). (c) Moon in Cancer (*c.* £300, 1982).

137. The Pharos lighthouse. (a) *Ae 28 mm, hemidrachma,* Hadrian. (b) *Ae 28 mm, hemidrachma,* Hadrian, but considerably worn (£15, 1979). (c) *Ae 35 mm, drachma,* Antoninus Pius, showing Isis Pharia catching the wind in a billowing sail and the lighthouse in the background.

Bronze coins of several second-century emperors feature the Pharos lighthouse, a wonder of the ancient world and still the standard word for a lighthouse in many European languages (Fig. 137). It was built on an island outside Alexandria harbour, sometime in the early third century BC. Soaring to a great height, (some sources say 100 metres, others say 160 metres,) this fortified lighthouse-cum-observation post mirrored a beacon reputedly visible from thirty-five miles. The coins show the square tower and lantern in some detail, the later engravings depicting the entrance a stage higher than previously – due either to rebuilding, artist's licence or simply the view from the other side! Two tritons (mermen) with conch-horns flank the lantern; a statue crowns the pinnacle. Even in worn condition the coin commands a price since it appears to be a fairly accurate representation. The legendary building toppled in an earthquake but its remains were still visible as late as the time of the Crusades. A fort now occupies the site.

Besides enjoying the price and condition of some of these coins, the collector can also make interesting use of his home library with the coins of Roman Egypt in front of him on the desk. One area has captured my interest. Nero's *tetradrachma* are commonly found. Some of them struck in AD 62–5 feature Poppaea, his second wife. From AD 66 to the Flavians they were struck for five emperors in succession on the authority of Tiberius Alexander, Prefect of Egypt and himself an Alexandrian Jew. An old question mark hangs over Poppaea – was she a Jewess? I would suggest that a new question mark could also be placed over Alexander – was Poppaea in some way his patron? The questions are both complex but they add to the interest of coins under discussion. Tacitus presents Poppaea as an adulteress and a schemer. Pliny Senior notes that she shod her mules with gold! Josephus Flavius, on the other hand, describes her as a 'God-fearing woman'. He hints at her more than passing interest in the Jews. She was kicked to death when pregnant during a domestic quarrel with Nero, her third husband, in AD 65 or possibly a little later. At her state funeral, in Nero's presence, her body was not cremated Roman-style, but spiced and sepulchred after the fashion of the east (and of the Jews) (Fig. 138).

She had become Nero's mistress about AD 58, while still married to Otho, her second husband. Her first marriage had been to the captain of Claudius' Praetorian Guard, about AD 45. She finally made the top rung of the social ladder, marrying Nero in AD 62. All of her marriages were contracted at court and to men in high office or esteem. Tiberius Alexander was also at court, certainly before AD 44, presented there by (Herod) Agrippa I, a friend of his father. In AD 46 Alexander was appointed by Claudius as Procurator of Judea, apparently a sensible compromise all round. Besides Alexander, there were other Jews at court, at least in Nero's day. One was a favourite actor. Josephus Flavius himself on a Judean delegation to Rome in AD 64 was flattered by attention and gifts from Poppaea. She also gave the whole delegation her support which, as *Augusta*, mattered a great deal. Suetonius notes that she was Nero's close counsellor.

Felix, Procurator of Judea AD 52–60 (see Ch. VII), had been a freedman at the court of Claudius, along with his brother Pallas who was Claudius' finance minister. Claudius' court had almost been taken over by ambitious freedmen. In Nero's day it was a world of fawning

138. Poppaea features on the reverse of a *tetradrachmon*, Nero, Year Eleven (AD 65), the year of her death. While her amber-dyed hair was a matter of comment among more traditionally minded Romans, she was best known for her skilful manipulation of Nero, including pressure on him to kill both his mother and his previous wife (£12, 1979).

knights – one reason for the Jewish unrest which erupted in revolt was the quality of Nero's appointments to Judea. Felix had married the Jewess Drusilla, sister of the young (Marcus) Agrippa II. In AD 60 they were both back in Rome, recalled from Judea in favour of Procurator Porcius Festus. Poppaea had been long enough at court to know her companions and to know her own mind. She took the side of a Jewish delegation in AD 62, against both Festus and Agrippa II, in an appeal over Agrippa's new dining-room window in Jerusalem! When Festus died in office that same year, Poppaea was instrumental in putting Florus into the post. His wife was a close friend.

Even more interesting, Paul the Judeo-Christian missionary was in Rome at this time under house arrest. He also was appealing to Nero. He would have been regarded as a Jew, albeit from a splinter group. According to the *Acts of the Apostles*, Procurator Felix had taken an interest in Paul at Caesarea and in the new religion he preached, 'the Way' as it was called. Did Poppaea meet Paul or influence his case? Paul's eventual appeal in AD 62–3 seems to have succeeded. In the light of Suetonius' comment and Paul's own written mention of 'brethren in Caesar's household' there may be an unrecorded story behind the story.

After the great fire of Rome in AD 64 Nero did not try to blame the city's Jews, an easy and popular scapegoat. Instead, he blamed the small breakaway sect of Christ-followers, many of them, like Peter the Galilean, Jewish. Was Poppaea's restraining hand at work here? Was she also linked to the eventual appointment in May AD 66 of Tiberius Alexander as Prefect of Egypt? Her bust appears on the Egyptian coins before his period of office. If her Jewish interests were well known, the design may have had some appeal in a city which hosted the largest Jewish colony outside Palestine, estimated at more than 100,000. It was not enough, however, to pre-empt a Jewish riot in Alexandria in AD 66 which the newly arrived Alexander put down with great bloodshed.

Alexander went on to hail first Galba, then Vespasian as the messiah, but he did not omit to strike coins of Otho and Vitellius to order. In AD 70 he was seconded to Titus' staff for the siege of Jerusalem. There was even a statue of him erected in Rome after his death. Juvenal, acid as ever, suggested that it would make a good urinal. Alexander was certainly an opportunist with a great capacity for spotting new messiahs and then placing himself at their right hands. I have already discussed the game of musical chairs played by his Alexandrian mint – eight months for Galba, three months for Otho, one month for Vitellius, then hastily on to Vespasian. Poppaea too may have been won over by his sense of timing. Both characters are good examples of the biographical side roads which a collector might choose to explore.

Britannia

Many collectors find themselves drawn to a brief period of Britain's history (AD 287–96) when the island was ruled by usurper emperors. The coins of Carausius and Allectus are found in some profusion in England, particularly with the advent of the metal detector. They are rarely found on the European mainland at all. Besides good silver *denarii*, a bold move ahead of its time to establish confidence, they also include large *antoniniani* almost the size of the *folles* soon to appear under Diocletian and a strange emergency issue known as the 'galley quinarius' of Allectus.

Britain was a Roman province from the Claudian invasion of AD 43 until about AD 410, when Honorius evacuated the remains of the island garrison. There may have been a brief return of a skeletal Roman administration a few years later, but from around that date the Romano-British society was left largely to fend for itself against Germanic raiders and settlers. The best known names from this twilight period – Maximus, Pelagius, Patricius and Artorius – owe far more to Rome than do our homely British versions Macsen, Peleg, Patrick and Arthur (Fig. 139).

Julius Caesar had reconnoitred Britain and a century later Claudius himself supervised the operations on the island. Shortly before this, Gaius 'Caligula' had marched troops as far as the Boulogne coast where he then appears to have made them collect shells in their helmets and march back again – Hitler's aborted 'Sea Lion' operation in 1940 had its precedent. Claudius' final successful and lasting occupation of

139. *Solidus*, Magnus Maximus, AD 383–8 (see Fig. 146), Macsen Wledig of early Welsh history. There is reason to believe that his wife Helena as well as some of his troops came from the Welsh base *Segontium* (Caernarfon). He has earned a place in the history of the Britons despite the facts that his stay was brief, that he was Spanish and an usurper.

Britain also owed something to a talented young legionary commander whose name was later to become a legend – Vespasian.

Twenty years after the invasion, the native queen Boudicca earned a place for herself in history by routing the Romans and putting Colchester, St Albans and London to the torch. Her nineteenth-century statue outside the Palace of Westminster suggests an independence of the Continental mainland which her Latin counterpart, Britannia, does not. Understandably, Nero's coins do not mark the event, a humiliation for Roman arms. The thick bands of ash still being found by archaeologists working on the sites of the burnt cities speak for themselves.

Around AD 119 the 'lost' Legion IX *Hispana* 'disappeared' from its base at York. This was long held due to massacre or corporate cashiering and the supposed 'event' fuelled the imagination of many writers. It may have simply been subject to a routine redeployment to the Rhine and then to face the Bar 'Kochba' revolt in Palestine.

The military crisis in the north at that period certainly prompted Hadrian's inspection shortly afterwards and the building of the famous Wall. One *sestertius* from the Army series (see Fig. 17) depicts troops of the British garrison being addressed by Hadrian. The Wall (*vallum*) is recorded only in the *Historia Augusta* but it may well be represented by the layered stones on second century *Britannia* coins (Fig. 140).

Many future emperors were blooded in Britain, as Vespasian had been. These included 'Caracalla' and Geta, Constantius I, Constantine and Theodosius I, who accompanied his father in AD 367. *Britannicus* was given as a name by Claudius to his son to mark the successful invasion and it came to be adopted as a title by emperors who campaigned there (Fig. 141). It is understandably prized by collectors.

The island also produced its own fair share of emperors, pretenders and outright rebels. For a short time its African governor, Clodius Albinus, was both a rival and a co-regent with Severus; in AD 190 he had succeeded Pertinax in the *Britannia* command. 'Caracalla' and Geta both assumed the purple from York after their father's death there

140. *As*, Antoninus Pius, AD 138–61, Britannia on the rocks. It may refer to the Wall, or as some suggest, the Antonine barricade of turf and rocks further north: it could simply stand for an island. The revived figure has featured on English coins since the seventeenth century, despite its European overtones and origin (£50, 1980).

141. *Denarius*, 'Caracalla', AD 211, struck within months of his father's death and his own accession at York. Note the title **BRIT(annicus)** and the figure of Victory referring to the recent campaigns in the north of Britain conducted by Severus and his two sons (£5, 1967).

in AD 211. The pretenders Carausius and Allectus made the province into an offshore military base against the Continental Empire. In the later years of the fourth century, Magnus Maximus, well known to students of Welsh lore and readers of Kipling, proclaimed himself emperor from the island before invading the Continent.

Roman rule effectively ended at the Wall. Shortlived and possibly misguided attempts were made to subdue Scotland, evidenced by the Antonine barricade further north. Ireland was never invaded or settled by the Romans, as far as we know, although Patricius its apostle was of Romano-British society. Wales was garrisoned. York and Chester were the main northern legionary depots. To the south of these, *Britannia Inferior* was residential, bristling with towns, roads, small ports, villas and farms.

When the Pope ordered the re-evangelisation of Britain in AD 596, he naturally designated London and York, the former civic and military centres, as the main bishoprics. Only the accident of Augustine's landing in Kent and the hospitable insistence of the Cantii gave their chief town to the English Church as its primatial see instead of London. York is the only other senior or arch-bishopric. Even a bishop's purple has its origin in the dress of the Imperial Prefects administering their *dioceses* across the later Empire. The history of Christianity in Roman Britain, however, is hardly known, consisting at the moment of scraps put together from archaeology and less reliable legendary traditions. Yet within memory-length of the reign of Hadrian a Christian writer, Minucius Felix, used Britain as 'proof' of God's providence and existence: the Gulf Stream poured in vital warmth from the sea to make up for the islanders' lack of sun. It did little for Veranius, one of Nero's governors of Britain who died of pneumonia and whose tomb on the Via Appia, near Rome, now basks in the sunshine he missed.

Coinage in the main came from the Continent. In the aftermath of the invasion local copies, some possibly struck by the legions themselves, were made of Claudian bronzes to meet the demands of the new

142. *Asses*, Claudius, AD 41–54. (a) Imperial coin, Minerva with Gorgon shield
(£4, 1980). (b) British copy, poor grade. Such copies are believed to have
formed up to 20 per cent of the total coin in circulation (£2, 1980). (See
Fig. 80).

provincial organisation (Fig. 142). These can be bought quite cheaply
and form a collection of particular interest even if artistry is lacking.
Again in the third century, copies were made of *antoniniani* (known as
'barbarous radiates') to meet the demand for coin caused by inflation
and debasement. How official these were is still a matter for debate.

The most dramatic and perhaps, for the collector, the most interesting period of all is that dating from the seizure of the province by
the admiral of the Roman Channel Fleet around AD 287. Marcus
Carausius, a Belgic Gaul (or *Menapian*, which could indicate British or
Manx links) set up what one authority has aptly called 'the first British
Empire'. He had good precedent in the rule of the usurper Postumus
(AD 259–68) over Britain, Germany and Gaul and he seems to have
taken note of Postumus' propaganda use of good coin (Fig. 143). After
a crude start Britain began to produce coin of a distinctly high quality,
beyond any comparison with the 'barbarous' copies then in circulation
and even exceeding the good but rough-hewn official Gallic coins of
the kind found in the Bath Hoard (see Fig. 40).

143. *Antoniniani*, Carausius, AD 287–93. (a) Earlier strikings, omitting title **C(aesar)**, before *c.* AD 290 (£100, 1982 and £7, 1980 respectively). (b) Later portraits with title **C(aesar)**. (£100, 1982, and £4, 1981 respectively).

Carausius had been based at *Gesoriacum* (Boulogne). He worked under Maximian who was created western *Augustus* in AD 286 and he seems to have combined piracy with his patrol duties. Either fear at being brought to book or jealousy of Maximian's new status caused him to rebel. His new coins quickly sported the titles **IMP(erator)** and **AUG(ustus)** and his bust wore the radiate crown. What are thought to be his earlier coins omit the title **C(aesar)**.

Carausius ruled Britain for six years. He founded or at least regularised an official mint in London which continued production for several decades after the end of this brief independence in AD 296. Under overall supervision of his finance minister and eventual successor, Allectus, the mint may have been in a temple of Juno Moneta by the present north wall of the Tower of London, near the site occupied until recently by the Royal Mint. The evidence is slender. It may have been quite large since it used a number of workshop letters but these have not yet been deciphered. Another mint was set up at **C** or **CL**, long thought to be Colchester (*Camulodunum*) but now felt more likely to be the naval base of Bitterne (*Clausentum* or *Classis*).

It would appear that around AD 290 Carausius did assume the title **Caesar** when it was clear that there was no chance of reconciliation with the *Tetrarchi* ('Four Rulers' – Diocletian, Maximian, Constantius and Galerius) of the mainland Empire. On some of his coins he even pictured the two *Augusti* as his co-rulers. Once Constantius was made Caesar in the West, AD 293, Carausius' hopes and claims were dashed.

Although Carausius neither started nor finished the building of the Saxon Shore forts to counter Saxon pirates, he continued their con-

struction. His fleet was the waterborne section of the line, covering
Channel approaches. In AD 293 he was murdered and succeeded by
Allectus, his finance minister. Allectus issued a high standard of coin
and continued to use it to proclaim his Imperial titles along with peace,
plenty and legionary loyalty on the reverses. The portraits, like those
of Carausius, would have been personally approved likenesses. The
mintmarks, still a novelty in Roman Britain, might have inspired confidence. It is these more than anything which attract the collector
(Fig. 144).

Allectus introduced a new bronze coin, known conventionally as 'quinarius' both because of its size and the letter **Q** accompanying the
mintmark (Fig. 145). The radiate crowned bust is usually the sign of
a double denomination – why then should it appear on a half such?
One theory is that this is emergency money, a final reduction of coin
metal in the last years of Allectus and like all such tokens 'redeemable
on the cessation of hostilities' for real money. The initial **Q** still
demands an explanation. It could just possibly be **Q(aestor)**, the rank
of a mint official and the authority for the issue of unusual coinage.
The galley on the reverse has trawled a few red herrings. Allectus
inherited the design from Carausius who in turn took it from Postumus'
magnificent double-*sestertii* – understandably, since the mainstay of
them all was the Channel fleet. There are several variations of ship.
Some show figures, either marines or commanders. These differences

144. The mintmarks of Carausius and Allectus: (a) **ML** (London) (b) **C** and
CL (Colchester or Fleet mints) (see Mints and mintmarks on p. 165).

145. The galleys of Allectus, showing clearly that the shorter vessel is designed by the artist to fit the space left by a longer legend (**Laetitia Aug.**). (See also Fig. 94.)

of detail, too minute to be of major impact on the public, are more likely to be individual engraver's licence than deliberate attempts to make some point. The two legends accompanying the ships – **Virtus** or **Laetitia** – are certainly abstract slogans traditionally associated with a speeding vessel as far back as the time of Hadrian. The theory that they may be the names of capital ships is attractive but fanciful.

In AD 296, under cover of a Channel fog, Constantius landed troops on the south coast while he took a fleet up the Thames. Allectus' forces met the main Roman army south-west of London. In pitched battle Allectus was killed and with him the short-lived independence of Britain. The coins of both usurpers tend to be found on sites as strays or if in hoards only in small numbers. For instance, the Bath Hoard (see Fig. 40) contained only two of Carausius and one of Allectus out of nearly 2,000 coins; the Penard Hoard had over eighty Carausian coins but these were mainly copies (see Fig. 38). On the other hand, droves of them are found in poor but recognisable condition on dealers' trays and in rummage boxes, brought up and cheapened by the metal detector.

It seems reasonable to assume that these coins were demonetised in AD 296. The whole Imperial currency was revamped around that time. The coinage of rebels and pretenders therefore fitted neither politically nor economically. Some coins even seem to bear signs of deliberate obliteration, the private citizen's attempt at *damnatio memoriae* (see Fig. 56b). Tradition has it that Allectus was a cruel ruler without the personality of Carausius.

London remained a mint city, issuing coin of good standard for the Empire until AD 325–6 (Fig. 146a). The mint was then closed, although

146. (a) the standard London mintmark in full, under Constantine. These coins are naturally popular among collectors but tend to be priced as if the mintmark were a 'rarity'. In fact it is not – London poured out a volume of coin in its few decades of operation. (b) A possible later London mintmark, from a *solidus* of Magnus Maximus, AD 383–8 (see Fig. 139). The mark has been interpreted as **Gold from (Londinium) Aug(usta Trinobantia)**, a later title of honour bestowed on London. However, since Magnus spent so little time in Britain and so much on campaign in Gaul, it is highly likely that the alternative reading, **Gold from Aug(ustodunum)** in Gaul (Autun in modern France), is more accurate. (Estimate at auction, 1981, £7,500.)

Magnus Maximus may have reopened it for a few years with the mint-mark **AUG** (usta Trinobantia). By then, not only was Maximus' time running short but so too was Britain's as a Roman province. The last Roman coins after AD 400, apart from the silver which some Britons clipped and then carefully hoarded after the closure of the western mints, are small *Ae* 3 and *Ae* 4 of Honorius.

No collection of *Britannia* coins would be complete without a so-called *minimissimus*. The very sound of the name suggests mouselike versions of something Roman. For a long time scholars accepted, how-ever uneasily, that these coins were struck during the sub-Roman administration of Britain in the early fifth century. Recent research has placed them firmly in the economic crisis of the later fourth century. By AD 370 the supplies of metal to outposts of empire like Britain had dried up. Finances were in a state of chaos. There were not even suf-ficient coins around to fractionalise as in Fig. 147, yet some token of currency was still demanded. The result was doll-house money, *min-imissimi* as low as 2 mm in diameter, economising on bronze to an unbelievable degree (Fig. 148). Just as the 'radiate minims' of the third century were still notionally *antoniniani*, these minimal fourth century pieces were probably still technically *folles* and almost certainly used in barter by the bagful according to a rough scale of bag weights.

We have come a long way from the bold new coinage introduced by

147. The depression of the coinage: two fractionalised coins, 7 mm each, possibly quarter denominations, dating from the later years of the fourth century.

148. The demise of the coinage' '*minimissimi*' struck on flans sliced from cast rods. These were found at Lydney, Gloucestershire, under a patched floor. They seem to have been made *c.* AD 370–90 and literally used by the adjustable bag weight or *follis* much as a modern bank counts coins by the bag; relatively large compared with those of 2 mm which, when handled in bulk, run through the fingers like rough sand!

Augustus. A few decades after the last miserable Roman pieces had stopped circulating in Britain, the last western Emperor, Romulus Augustus, was derisively dubbed *Augustulus* or puny-Augustus. In the Rome of 1945 an Italian poet wrote of Mussolini's death, 'The second Romulus has ended up a second Remus overnight.' Augustus too had become Augustulus by the fifth century, but it had taken 500 years. Perhaps the tiny *minimissimus* and the shorn *siliquae* would make a fitting last page to any collection of Roman coin themes.

Postscript

This book began in the ruins of Rome. In every city of the Empire, from Antioch to Bath, the great monuments and public buildings suffered neglect. The cities were besieged and sacked, some several times in a single century. Broken marble facings and steps provided crude and terrifying missiles for the catapult; they were equally effective at close quarters when dropped from the walls. Marble was burnt to provide lime in cement mortar. In time, great buildings collapsed and no one felt responsible for them or capable of organising their repair. Some semblance of life did continue, even if only by cannibalising the luxuries and glories of a previous generation. Churches rather than temples were the focus of the spirit of what was left of Rome – the dressed stone passed from one to the other. Seats from the racing circus and the amphitheatre were taken for the basilicas; marble basins from the baths became the coffins of the exhumed martyrs; pillars of marble from every province of the Empire were sized and numbered to provide aisles; temples and tombs, once shelled, became churches and forts.

Floods and rains together blocked the drains and raised the ground level. Grass sprouted and compacted the mud produced by the over-flow of water. Silt from the rivers spread over the annual crop of grass, thereby producing more grass. Rubbish was tipped and debris was piled on ground once thought to have been tamed. Later generations gazed in awe at the size of the ruins and whispered that they had been 'the work of giants'. Amid all this chaos, only the tinier items slipped away to emerge centuries later as reminders of what had once been. Among them were the coins which we now collect.

PART III

COLLECTORS' WORKING INFORMATION

I. The Roman Augusti (including pretenders)

A = abdicated; B = battlefield death; DEH = died in enemy hands; E = executed; GOC = General Officer Commanding M = murdered; S = suicide.

Julio-Claudians

Augustus 27 BC–AD 14 (great nephew of J. Caesar)
Tiberius 14–37 (stepson and in-law of Augustus)
Gaius 'Caligula' 37–41 (adopted son of Tiberius) M
Claudius 41–54 (uncle of Gaius)?M
Nero 54–68 (nephew of Gaius) M

The four generals

Galba June 68–Jan. 69 (GOC Lower Spain)M
Otho Jan.–Apr. 69 (GOC Lusitania) S
Vitellius Jan.–Dec. 69 (GOC Lower Rhine) M

Vespasian July 69–79 (GOC Judea) ⎫
Titus 79–81 (son of Vespasian) ?M ⎬ *The Flavians*
Domitian 81–96 (son of Vespasian) M ⎭
Nerva 96–8 (civil and legal figure)
Trajan 98–117 (GOC Upper Germany, adopted by Nerva)
Hadrian 117–38 (Trajan's great nephew, adopted by Trajan)
Antoninus 'Pius' 138–61 (adopted by Hadrian)
M. Aurelius 161–80 (adopted by and son-in-law of Antoninus)
Commodus 177–92 (son and co-Augustus of Aurelius) M
Verus 161–9 (Antoninus' son-in-law and co-Augustus of Aurelius)

Year of the five

Pertinax 193 (Prefect of Rome, former GOC Britain)M
Didius Julianus 193 (senator who bought the office)M
Pescennius Niger 193–4 (GOC Syria) M
Clodius Albinus 193–5 (GOC Britain and Gaul; declared usurper 195–7) M

Septiminus Severus 193–211 (GOC Pannonia)

Geta 209–12 (son of Severus and co-Augustus) M
'Caracalla' 198–217 (son of Severus and co-Augustus) M *The Severans*
Macrinus 217–18 (African Prefect of Guard) E
Elagabalus 218–21 (great nephew of Severus) M
Severus Alexander 222–35 (cousin and adopted son of Elagabalus) M

Year of the six

Maximinus 235–8 (soldier) M
Gordian I 238 (Proconsul in Africa) S
Gordian II 238 (son of Gordian I and co-Augustus) B
Balbinus 238 (senator and co-Augustus with Pupienus) M
Pupienus 238 (senator and co-Augustus with Balbinus) M
Gordian III 238–44 (nephew and grandson of first two Gordians) M

Philip I 244–9 (Prefect of Guard) B (*Pacatian* 248 *Moesia*)
Philip II 247–9 (son and co-Augustus) B (*Jotapian* 248 *Syria*)

Year of the five

Trajan Decius 249–51 (GOC Moesia) B
Herennius Etruscus 251 (son of Trajan and co-Augustus) B
Hostilian 251 (surviving younger son of Trajan)
Trebonianus Gallus 251–3 (soldier) M
Volusian 251–3 (son and co-Augustus) M (*Aemilianus* 253 *Moesia*) M

Valerian I 253–60 (GOC Upper Rhine) DEH
Gallienus 253–68 (son of Valerian) M
Saloninus 259 (son of Gallienus) M

The Gallic Empire
(*Postumus* 259–68 *Gaul, Spain & Britain.*) M
(*Macrianus* 260–1 *as above*) B
(*Quietus* 260–1, *son*) B
(*Victorinus* 268–70, *son*) M
(*Tetricus I* 270–73, *son*) A
(*Tetricus II son*) A

Claudius 'Gothicus' II 268–70 (soldier)
Quintillus 270 (brother) s
Aurelian 270–5 (soldier) M (*Valabathus* 271–2 *Palmyra*)
Tacitus 275–6 (senator)
Florian 276 (half-brother) M
Probus 276–82 (soldier) M
Carus 282–3 (Prefect of Guard)
Numerian 283–4 (son of Carus) M
Carinus 283–4 (son and co-Augustus) M (*Julian* 285 *Pannonia*) B

Diocletian 284–305 (Prefect of Guard) A
Maximian 286–305/306–8/310 (soldier) M/?S (*Carausius* 287–93 *Britain*) M
Constantius I 305–6 (son-in-law of Max.) (*Allectus* 293–6 *Britain*) B
Galerius 305–11 (soldier)
Severus II 306–7 (soldier) E
Maximinus II 308–13 (related to Galerius)
Maxentius 306–12 (son of Maximian) B (*Alexander* 311 *Africa*) E
Licinius I 308–24 (co-Augustus with Const.) E
Constantine I 307–37 (son of Constantius I)
Constantine II 337–40 (son of Constantine) M
Constans 337–50 (son of Constantine) M
Constantius II 337–61 (son of Constantine) (*Magnentius* 350–53 *West*)
s (*Vetranio* 350 *Illyria*) A (*Nepotian* 350 *Rome*) M

Julian II 361–3 (nephew of Constantine) B
Jovian 363–4 (Prefect of Guard)
Valentinian I 364–75 (soldier) (*Procopius* 365–6 *Constantinople*) E
Valens 374–8 (brother and co-Augustus) B
Gratian 367/375–83 (son of Valentinian I) M
Valentinian II 375–92 (son of Valentinian I) M

Theodosius 379–95 (soldier) (*Magnus Maximus* 383–8 *The West*) E (*Flavius Victor, son*) E
Eugenius 392–4 (teacher and western puppet Emperor) E
Arcadius 395–408 (son of Theodosius) E
Honorius 393–423 (son of Theodosius) (*Constantine III* 407–11 *Britain*)
E (*Constans* 408–11 *Britain, son*) E

The fifth century AD is best described by the single word chaos. Rome was sacked by the Visigoths under Alaric in AD 410, the Vandals under Gaiseric in AD 455 and again by the Goths in AD 472. Understandably, by then it had virtually ceased to be the western capital which had been withdrawn to Ravenna. The west distintegrated, the east held firm and in AD 476 the Emperor at Constantinople reverted to sole rule of the remains of the Roman Empire. In the west his rule was nominal.

II. Imperial titles and offices

AUGUSTUS   The title given by Rome to Octavian, literally 'auspicious one' or 'great one'. It was exclusive to the Emperor (and his consort as **AUGUSTA.**). From this is derived the month name **August**, which also follows the month name after **Julius** Caesar, Octavian's adoptive father.

CAESAR   The family name maintained by the descendants of Julius **Caesar**. When the family line died out with Nero in AD 68, it became a title for emperors and their heirs. Vitellius (AD 69) and Carausius (British usurper AD 287–93) were reluctant to use this revered title and assumed it only late in their reigns. **Czar, Tsar** and **Kaiser** are derived from this, deliberately assumed for their imperial overtones. **Caesarean** also has the same root: Julius Caesar was said to have been born in this manner.

CENSOR(ia)
POT(estas)
PER(petua)   The old Republican office of **Censor**, as the name implies, had responsibility for records of citizenship and **censuses**. More important, the office carried an ancient right to fix the list of the members of the Senate and of the classes, to include and to expel from both. Domitian, who assumed the title for life, was the last to use it.

CO(n)S(ul)   The chief magistrates of the Republic were the two **consuls** who held office for one year. The emperor frequently held the office along with an associate. Dates can be worked out from a stated number of renewals of office. Sometimes **DESIGNAT(us)** – consul elect, or **ITER** – consul again, is added to the title. The modern diplomat of that rank is so named as the chief representative official for certain matters in part of a foreign country.

DIVUS   'Deified', 'assumed into the company of the gods', 'divine'. The honour was reflected on to the living relatives who might assume the title **DIVI F(ilius)**, 'son of the divine'. In later centuries the title passed from the Emperor to Christ in the form of the technical doctrinal description, 'Son of God'.

D(ominus)
N(oster)
'Our Master', 'our Lord' a title found on Imperial coins from the time of Diocletian (AD 286–305) which later became a liturgical and doctrinal description of Christ.

IMPERATOR
'Commander-in-Chief', much as the US President or British monarch commands the Forces. The man who held the legions thereby held the throne. When used of heirs to the throne (Caesars), it takes on the meaning of 'deputy commander'. From this title denoting the real source of the Roman ruler's power come the words **imperial** and of course **emperor**.

NOB(ilis)
'Noble', found on later Imperial coins which depict a Caesar rather than the emperor himself. It carries the hint of 'Highness' rather than 'Majesty'.

P(ius)
F(elix)
'Reverend and blessed' found on Imperial coins from the time of M. Aurelius (AD 161–80) in abbreviated form, a description of the named emperor.

PONT(ifex)
MAX(imus)
'Highest priest' of the gods of Rome. This ancient office was taken up along with many others by the emperor. **Pontifex** literally means 'bridgebuilder' between gods and men. The title was later assumed by the Bishop of Rome in his role as *Papa* or Father-bishop – **Supreme Pontiff**.

P(ater)
P(atriae)
'Father of his country', a regular Imperial title of honour.

TRIB(unicia)
POT(estas)
Under the Republic the **Tribune** was the people's champion and spokesman, sometimes the scourge of the Senate. Dates can be worked out from a stated number of renewals of this power, held afresh each year by the emperor. From this is derived **tribunal**, a public court of enquiry or appeal.

Personal names

TIberius, CLAUDius and **DOMITianus** are personal names. Double names indicate a relationship, as for instance, **NERO CLAUDius** (Nero), **TIberius CLAUDius** (Claudius) and **Titus VESPASIANus** (Titus). 'Caligula' (Little Combat Boots) and 'Caracalla' (Little Greatcoat) are nicknames, not found on coins or inscriptions. **Gaius** is an alternative pronunciation of **Caius**, hence abbreviated **C**. Many emperors had the same name – there were two **Trajans** and two **Claudius**, three **Constantines** and three **Constantius** among many others.

The name **ANTONINUS** causes much confusion since it was used by five emperors as a family name. **Antoninus Pius** was the first and is readily distinguished by the title '*Pius*' as well as the portrait. **Marcus Aurelius** also used the name but with his personal names preceding it and without the title. **Commodus** used it, but prefixed it with his own names and followed it with the title '**Pius**'. 'Caracalla' and **Elagabalus** used the same name and title as the first **Antoninus** and their coins are distinguishable by portrait, style and occasional additions to the title such as **BRIT**. or a personal name.

Campaign titles

GERManicus, PARTHicus, ARMENiacus, DACicus, BRITannicus and **GOTHicus**, among others, were bestowed on the Emperor for a feat of arms against Rome's enemies. It should be remembered that the emperor was primarily Imperator-in-Chief or Supremo. The custom of awarding such titles still obtained in Britain after 1945, as for example, Mountbatten of Burma and Alexander of Tunis.

III. Mints and mintmarks

The earlier Roman mintmarks were marks of authority rather than of location, e.g. **SC** and/or the name of a moneyer. In the first two centuries AD several mints struck Imperial coinage besides that of the city of Rome – but only periodically. Style of engraving and the occasional obvious mark such as the 'globe' at the tip of the neck on coins from a western mint (thought to be Lyons) give some clue as to origin.

By the third century, due to the sheer size of territory to be administered, to local needs and to the demands of rebel generals, mints mushroomed across the Empire. Around AD 294 under Diocletian's money reforms, Imperial coinage began to follow a standard pattern both in design and in quality of metal. Each official mint was required to place on its products a recognised Latin abbreviation for the name of the city, although in some cases the Greek **K** proved stronger than the Latin **C**. Depending on the size of the mint the particular workshop might also be indicated either in Latin letters (**P(rima), S(secunda), T(ertia)**etc) or in the Greek numeral alphabet ($A = 1$, $B = 2$, $\Gamma = 3$ etc). Out of traditional respect, the location mark might be prefixed or suffixed by **P(ecunia)** or **S(acra) M(oneta)** or even simply **M(oneta)**.

After AD 367 Imperial taxes were collected in bullion form carrying an assay mark, rather than in coin which might be adulterated. Coins were then struck from the bullion collected and in turn began to carry a form of assay mark to vouch for their fineness. Silver carried the letters **P(u)S(ulatum)**. meaning literally 'blistered' or 'refined by fire'; gold carried the letters **OB(ryzum)**, the Greek word for 'assayed' or 'fire-tested'. The assayer of the mint (*Comes*) also added to the gold his title **COM**. This new quality-control mark is found sometimes after the mintmark, sometimes displacing it completely from the exergue (Fig. 149).

Commonly encountered fourth century mintmarks:

AL(E) – *Alexandria Magna, Aegyptus* (Alexandria, Egypt).
AMB(I) – *Civitas Ambianorum, Gallia Belgica* (Amiens, France).

149. A selection of mintmarks: (for clarity the mint name is left with ending unchanged) (a) CON(stantinopolis) OB(ryzum). (b) R(a)V(enna) COM(es) OB(ryziacus). (c) AQ(uileia) P(u)S(ulatum). (d) LUG(dunum). (e) T(he)S(alonika) A(Officina 1). (f) S(acra) M(oneta) T(h)ES(salonika). (g) M(oneta) OST(ia) A (Officina I). (h) S(acra) M(oneta) H(eraclea) T(hracica) S(ecunda Officina). (i) S(acra) M(oneta) ANT(iochia). (j) P(ecunia) L(o)N-(dinium). (k) S(acra) M(oneta) N(ico)M(edia). (1) S(acra) M(oneta) N(icomedia) B (Officina 2). (m) S(ecunda Officina) CONS(tantinopolis). (n) TR(everi) OB(ryzum). (o) P(ecunia) T(icinum) (p) 3rd (Officina) SIS(cia). A, H, K, M, N and R can easily be confused in later engraving. A compacted M can be mistaken for an N; an opentop A or a badly defined K for an H.

AN(T) – *Antiochia, Syria* (Antakya, S. Turkey)

AQ(VIL) – *Aquileia, Pannonia* (ruins at Aglar, near Trieste).

A(R)(L) – *Arelas/Arelate, Gallia Narbonensis* (Arles, France)

AVG – possibly *Londinium*, renamed *Augusta Trinobantium* mid-fourth century, but likely *Augustodunum, Gallia Lugdunensis* (Autun, France).

C(L) – uncertain British mint under Carausius and Allectus – *?Camulodunum* (Colchester); *?Clausentum* (Bitterne); *?Classis* (Naval Mint).

C(ON)(S) – *Constantinopolis, Thracia* (Stamboul, Turkey).

CON(ST) – *Constantina Gallia* (new town extension to *Arelas, Gallia*).

CVZ(IC)(EN) – *Cyzicus, Asia* (ruins at Balkiz, Kapi Dagi, Turkey).

H(ER)(ACL) – *Heraclea Thracica.* (Menelik, Turkey).

K(ART) – *Carthago Nova, Africa* (ruins near Tunis, Tunisia).

L(O)(N) – *Londinium, Britannia* (London, Britain).

L(V)(G)(D) – *Lugdunum, Gallia Lugdunensis* (Lyons, France)

M(E)D – *Mediolanum, Italia* (Milan, Italy).

N(IK)(O) – *Nicomedia, Bithynia* (ruins near Izmit, Turkey).

OST – *Ostia, Italia* (ruined port town near Rome, now inland).

R – uncertain mint under Carausius and Allectus *?Rotomagus* (Rouen).

RSR – uncertain mint under Carausius and Allectus *?Rationalis Summarum Rerum* (Chief Finance Officer).

R(A)V – *Ravenna, Gallia Cisalpina* (Ravenna, Italy).

R(O)(M)(A) – *Roma, Italia* (Rome, Italy).

S(ER)(D) – *Serdica, Dacia/Moesia* (Sofia, Bulgaria).

SIR(M) – *Sirmium, Pannonia/Illyricum* (Sremska Mitrovicz, Jugoslavia).

S(IS)(C) – *Siscia Flavia-Severa, Pannonia* (Siszek, Jugoslavia).

TR(E) – *Augusta Treverorum, Gallia Belgica* (Trier, Germany).

T(H)(E)(S) – *Thessalonika, Macedonia* (Thessaloniki, Greece).

T – *Ticinum, Italia* (Pavia, Italy).

VR(B) – *Urbs Roma* (City of Rome).

NB – **COMOB** – *Comes Obryziacus* (Count of Gold, or Imperial Assayer).

   CONOB – *Constantinopolis Obryzum* (gold struck at Constantinople).

IV. The Roman denominations

The names of many later Imperial denominations are unknown, as are the relationships between them. Modern methods of metal analysis have provided partial answers to some questions posed by Roman currency. Much is still speculation. It should be noted that units and apparent submultiples such as the *solidus* and *semissis* are not necessarily in a fixed relationship to each other. Nor does the end of production of a denomination mean that it goes out of circulation.

GOLD

Double-aureus (modern name) – introduced by 'Caracalla' in AD 215; dropped after his death, again introduced by Trajan Decius, AD 250; issued from time to time over the remaining half-century. A 'radiate' coin, multiple of the *aureus*.

Aureus – rarely struck under the Republic until Caesar's political lifetime; basic regular gold unit of Imperial currency from the time of Augustus; succeeded by unit known as the *solidus* early in the reign of Constantine I, which continued into Byzantine times, known universally in the Middle Ages as the gold *bezant*.

Quinarius in gold – approximately half the gold Imperial currency unit, issued sporadically; the smaller gold denomination of the fourth century was known as the *semissis*, although not necessarily a strict *half-solidus*.

Tremissis – a late fourth-century denomination, the smallest in gold; an earlier gold piece approximating to nine *siliquae* in value has been variously dubbed *tremissis, triens* and *scripulum*, the latter being a contemporary nickname for tiny coins of both gold and silver, hence the word 'scruple'.

SILVER

Double-denarius (modern name) – better known in modern parlance as the *antoninianus* (after Marcus Aurelius Antoninus 'Caracalla' who introduced it, AD 214.) A 'radiate' coin, it may have been known to contemporaries as the *radiatus*; discontinued after the death of Elagabalus, AD 222, possibly in part reaction against his obsessive sun religion; revived AD 238 by the co-Emperors Balbinus and Pupienus. Increasingly debased and diminished, it survived in one form or another efforts by Aurelian, Probus and even Diocletian to reform the currency. The 'radiate' (*XXI*) disappeared after the beginning of the fourth century. The *miliarensis* (relatively modern name) or multiple of the *siliqua* was struck in the fourth century in 'light' and 'heavy' versions and may be considered a technical if distant successor of the *denarius* multiple or *antoninianus* of 'Caracalla'.

Denarius – the longest surviving denomination, backbone of Republican and Imperial currency from before 200 BC to *c*. AD 238, after which it was issued more sporadically and finally in debased bronze. At the end of the third century its successor the *argenteus* (relatively modern name taken from the late Roman word for silver-coin-in-general) was introduced, to be replaced (or renamed?) by the *siliqua* (contemporary name? meaning literally a 'bean') within thirty years. The so-called *argenteus* may in fact have been known as *siliqua* from the start.

Quinarius or *half-denarius* – issued more or less regularly in parallel with the *denarius*; its distant fourth-century successor may have been called the *half-siliqua*.

Sestertius – under the Republic, a silver *quarter-denarius* issued only sporadically until the emergence in 23 BC of a large orichalcum coin of the same name.

BRONZE *(including billon, orichalcum and copper)*

Double-sestertius (modern name) – issued by Trajan Decius, AD 250, and sporadically after his reign until the last issued by the usurper Postumus in northern Europe *c*. AD 265. A 'radiate' large bronze, it is assumed to be double the value of a third-century *sestertius*, partly because of this interpretation of the radiate crown, partly because it was struck on good rounded flans of the previous centuries. At the least it seems to have been a multiple of the *sestertius*.

Sestertius – the name of the smallest silver coin of the Republic passed to large coins of orichalcum introduced by Augustus. Its zinc alloy degenerated into copper-bronze before the coin disappeared in the reigns of Gallienus and the usurper Postumus.

Dupondius, double-as or *half-sestertius* – issued in orichalcum in parallel with the *sestertius* and *as* in Imperial times; a 'radiate' coin from the time of the Flavians.

As – the original base metal unit of the Republic, it sank from 1 lb to 0.5 oz. in weight before being discontinued in 82 BC. The name was handed on to the low copper denomination of the Empire; Nero and Trajan experimented with orichalcum *asses*; the pure copper had given way to copper-bronze by the end of the first century AD. The coin disappeared with its multiples, the *sestertius* and *dupondius*.

Follis (retrospective post-contemporary name?) – the billon, silver-plated coin of the size of the old *as* introduced AD 294, apparently the successor to the *XXI* coins of Aurelian; within three decades it declined to a quarter its original size. The name originally denoted a 'purse' or 'leather money bag' and by transference came to mean 'purse money', 'small change' or 'bagfull'. About AD 318 another bronze coin (*Ae 3*) was introduced with a minimal (unintentional?) silver content, modelled on old *argenteus* patterns and replacing the shrunken *follis*; it may have been known as a *centenionalis*. About AD 348 another *centenionalis* of bronze (*Ae 2*) was introduced, better known during its short life as *pecunia maiorina*. It was closely followed by an even shorter-lived *double-centenionalis* (e.g. the famous *Chi-Rho* type of Magnentius). A decade or so later, Julian II revived the old billon *follis* (known more commonly today as an *Ae 1*) in a last brief curtaincall for the traditions of Roman coining. Despite these efforts, only the small *Ae 3* and *Ae 4* survived by the end of the fourth century, the base metal successors of the old reduced *follis*.

Semis, or *half-as* – struck under the Republic until 82 BC when the *as* and its fractions were discontinued. Augustus revived the denomination which was struck increasingly sporadically until its last revival under Trajan Decius; some of Trajan I's *semisses* are 'radiate' coins.

Quadrans or *quarter-as* – struck in parallel with the *semis*; last issue in the closing decade of the second century AD.

Fractions of the as below *quadrans* value were issued under the Republic until 82 BC but with increasing irregularity – *triens* (one third), *sextans* (one sixth), *uncia* (one twelfth), *semuncia* (half *uncia*) and *quartuncia* (quarter *uncia*); none of these denominations was revived in the Imperial period.

Minimus – modern term of convenience, akin to the language of music, denoting the tiniest coins of the later Empire less than 12 mm diameter. There seem to have been two main periods of *minimus* production: 'radiate minims' or miniature *antoniniani* were manufactured *c*. AD 270, the nadir of the debased *antoninianus*; in a similar period of economic strain a century later, *minimi* and fractional clippings came into circulation, including the celebrated 2 mm *minimissimi*, probably used in transaction by the adjustable bag-weight or *follis*. Despite popular belief, the evidence places them firmly within the final period of Roman rule in Britain rather than in some later 'twilight' civilisation.

V. Latin and Greek simplified

Latin nouns and accompanying adjectives are constructed upon a basic stem (which itself sometimes varies). Onto this stem are added twelve possible endings; six for the singular and six for the plural. Which of the six is employed depends on the place of the word in the sentence (subject or object or addressee in direct speech); other endings take the place of *to*, *by* and *of* in English. Latin and Greek nouns and adjectives also have a gender (masculine, feminine, neuter), and there are different sets of endings corresponding to these. Many Roman coins carry a dedicatory ending to the words; e.g. *Optimo Principi* = 'to the finest prince'. Many words are abbreviated, limited by coin space. Many others which have ordinary meanings are also the names of personifications and deities concerned with that particular object; e.g. *Ceres* = corn or grain, but it is also the name of the grain goddess. Where the stem itself varies on the coins, the variation is shown in brackets.

Abundantia – plenty; prosperity – usually personified.

Adlocutio(n-) – formal address, usually to troops.

Adventus – approach or return-in-state, hence **Advent** before Christmas.

Aequita(s/t–) – fairness; justice; equity – usually personified.

Aetern–(adj.) – eternal.   **Aeternita(s/t–)** – eternity.

Alimentum – food supply – usually personified.

Amor – love.

Annona – grain supply – usually personified.

Bon–(adj.) – good; fortunate; happy, hence **bonus** means extra for good work.

C(a)elest–(adj.) – heavenly; to do with the sky.

Capta – conquered; subjected.

Carita(s/t-) – love; care.

Castra – army camp.

Ceres – grain; cereals – usually personified.

Certamina – games; sporting competitions.

Cives – citizens.

Civita(s/t–) – the state; a city authority.

Clementia – mercy; care; kindness – usually personified.

Cohor(s/t) – battalion.

Colonia – settlement of military veterans.

Com(es/it) companion; ally, later title of honour, 'count'.

Concordia – harmony; agreement – usually personified.

Conditor – founder.

Consensus – agreement.

Consecratio(n–) – dedication; deification, usually on posthumous coins.

Conservator – saviour; preserver; protector.

Conservatrix – feminine.

Constantia – steadfastness; courage, – usually personified.

Custo(s/d–) – guardian; sentry.

Dat-(adj.) – given; bestowed upon; granted to.

De – about; concerning; over (as in a victory).

Decenn(alia) – ten-yearly.

Decursio – military exercises; manoeuvres.

Designat-(adj.) – elect; designate.

Deus – god.

Devict-(adj.) – subjected; defeated; conquered.

Equites – the class of knights.

Eventus – outcome; result; omen.

Exercitus – army.

Expeditio – departure-in-state; tour; campaign tour.

Fecundita(s/t–) – fruitfulness; fertility – usually personified.

Felicita(s/t) – blessedness; happiness – usually personified.

Feli(x/c–) – blessed; happy.

Fides – confidence; loyalty; trust – usually personified.

Filius – son.   **Filia** – daughter.

Fiscus – tax.

Fortuna – good fortune; prosperity – usually personified.

Frumentum – harvest; crop; grain.

Frugifer–(adj.) – fruitful; fertile; cropbearing.

Fundator – founder; supporter.

Gaudium – joy; rejoicing.

Gen(us/er–) – race, usually the human race.

Genetri(x/c-) – begetter of; lifegiving; mother.

Genius – spirit; mind – usually personified.

Gloria – glory; honour; reputation.

Hilarita(s/t–) – good heart; rejoicing – usually personified.

Hono(s/r–) – honour; reputation; high standing.

Human–(adj.)– human.

Indulgentia – mercy; kindness; pity – usually personified.

Invict-(adj.) – unconquerable; unconquered.

Iovis – Jove; Jupiter.

Iustitia – justice – usually personified.

Iuventu(s/t–) – youth; the young generation.

Laetitia – happiness; joy – usually personified.
Legio(n–) – legion; regiment.
Liberalita(s/t–) – public generosity – usually personified.
Liberator – liberator.
Liberta(s/t–) – freedom – usually personified.
Lucifer – lightbearing; day-star, later name for Devil by a misreading.
Lucina – light; day-star.
Mar(s/t–) – Mars, god of war.
Martial–(adj.) – military; to do with Mars.
Mat(er/r–) – mother.
Maxim–(adj.) – highest; greatest; largest.
Mil(es/it–) – soldier.
Moderatio(n–) – restraint; moderation – usually personified.
Moneta – money; mint; title of the goddess Juno.
Multa – public donatives, given on accessions and anniversaries.
Munificientia – generosity.
Nobilita(s/t–) – good birth; noble background – usually personified.
Nov–(adj.) – new.
Ob – for; because of.
Optim–(adj.) – best; finest; greatest.
Orbis – the world.
Orien(s/t–) – rising; eastern.
Pacator/Pacifer – pacifier; conqueror.
Pat(er/r–) – father.
Patria – homeland.
Pa(x/c–) – peace – usually personified.
Perpetuita(s/t–) – eternity; perpetuity.
Pieta(s/t–) – devotion; loyalty – usually personified.
Pius – venerable.
Pontif(ex/ic–) – priest; go-between; bridgebuilder.
Populus – the people.
Princ(eps/ip–) – first citizen; leader of state; prince.
Profection(n–) – setting out; state departure; expedition.
Propagator – parent; fruitbearer.
Propugnator – champion of; fighter for; defender.
Providentia – foresight; care; wisdom – usually personified.
Provincia – colony; province.
Pudicitia – modesty; womanliness – usually personified.
Quie(s/t–) – peace.
Quinquenn(alia) – five-yearly.
Recept–(adj.) – received; welcomed; accepted.
Rector – guide; controller; ruler.
Reduct–(adj.) – conquered; subjected; defeated.
Redu(x/c–) – restorer; guide.

Reipublica – the state; nation, literally the public business.
Reparatio(n–) – restoration.
Restitutor – rebuilder; restorer.   **Restitut–**(adj.)–restored.
Sacerdo(s/t–) – priest.
S(a)eculum – the age; the present time.   **S(a)ecular–**(adj.).
Salu(s/t–) – health; safety; wellbeing – usually personified.
Salutar–(adj.) – health/safety-bringing.   **Salvator** – saviour.
Sapientia – wisdom; knowledge.
Securita(s/t–) – safety; security; defence – usually personified.
Servat–(adj.) – made safe; defended; preserved.
Sid(us/er–) – star; heavens.
Signa – battle standards; regimental colours.
Sol – sun.
Solut–(adj.) – performed or taken (applied to vows).
Soror – sister.
SPQR – Senate and People of Rome.
Spes – hope – usually personified.
Stator – mainstay or rallyer of armies.
Suscept–(adj.) – performed or taken (applied to vows).
Temp(us/or–) – the time; the age.
Terra – land; earth; country.
Tranquillita(s/t–) – peace; calm; settled times.
Triumfator – conqueror; victor.
Tutator – saviour; preserver; defender.
Uberita(s/t–) – fruitfulness; fertility – usually personified.
Ubique – to all parts, sides; to everywhere.
Ultor – defender; avenger.
Undique – from all parts, sides; from everywhere.
Urbs – city, particularly Rome itself.
Vehiculatio(n–) – Imperial carrying service.
Victor – conqueror.
Victri(x/c–) – conqueress.
Victoria – victory – usually personified.
Virtu(s/t–)– strength; military steadfastness; courage.
Votum – vow; pledge; promise.
Vulcanus – Vulcan, god of fire and earth.

Basic Greek on coins

The Greek alphabet with English equivalents:
Α Β Γ Δ Ε Ζ Η Θ Ι Κ Λ Μ Ν Ξ Ο Π Ρ Σ/C Τ Υ Φ Χ Ψ Ω
A B G D E Z Ē Th I K L M N X O P R S T U Ph Ch Ps O
The Latin **V** is rendered **OY** in Greek; there is no letter **H** as such.

The letters of the alphabet with extra symbols inserted also serve as numerals:

A (1)   B (2)   Γ (3)   Δ (4)   E (5)   ς (6)   Z (7)   H (8)
Θ (9)   I (10)   K (20)   Λ (30)   M (40)   N (50)   Ξ (60)
O (70)   Π (80)   Φ (90)   P (100)   etc.

Where a number (sometimes even written out in full) is used for the calendar year it is preceded by a sign like an English **L** (sometimes the full word for a year, **ETOYC**, is used instead.) The symbol **L** is an ancient Egyptian year sign. The reckoning bases most frequently found are those calculated from the battle of Actium (31 BC), or from the first year of a particular emperor's reign. Some mintmarks also contain the number of the workshop expressed in the numerical alphabet.

The collector should know the following words on sight:

AYTOKPATŌP	– Autocrator	– Imperator
BAΣIΛEOC	– Basileos	– King
ΓEPM	– Germ(anicus)	
KAIΣAPOC	– Kaisaros	– Caesar
PΩMH	– Rome	
ΣEBAΣTOC	– Sebastos	– Augustus
XP (usually crossed)	Chr(ist)	

VI. Selection of numismatic terms

Au., Ar., Ae. (Latin; *aureum*, gold; *argentum*, silver; *aes*, bronze): sometimes expressed in monogram form, originally for the stonemason's convenience: *N; R* and *Æ*. It is also worth noting that besides the Roman *U* engraved like a *V*, there is no letter *J* in Latin, simply an *I* pronounced as *Y*.

Barbarous: description frequently applied to the cruder contemporary imitations of Roman coins to indicate their provincial or non-Roman origin. *Barbarus* is a Greek word, taken over by the Romans to describe foreigners who spoke in other (unintelligible) languages. They seemed to be mouthing sheep-sounds, or 'bar-bar', hence the name. Today it carries in English overtones of crudity and violence, rather like the words 'pagan' and 'heathen' (formerly the words for 'man from the countryside' and 'man from the moorlands').

Billon (Old French: lump or base metal): technically applied to any silver coin containing more than 50 per cent alloy, usually copper. The term has a wider, popular use covering any debased silver. A billon silver coin containing more than 75 per cent copper is technically **black billon**. Much of the so-called bronze *follis* money of the earlier fourth century is in fact silver-coated **billon.**

Brockage: (*broken*) a coin which has been struck in relief on one side, usually the obverse side face down on the anvil die, and incuse on the other side, due to a previously struck coin sticking to the upper or punch die. In effect, the incuse design is a mirror matrix of the relief design. In some cases this effect may not be produced by accident but by design as a commemorative piece (see Fig. 105).

Coin (Latin: *cuneus*, wedge; French: *coin*, angle or corner): the name probably derives by transference from the wedge-shape of the upper or punch-die used in hand striking of coin.

Countermark: letter or symbol punched into a reheated coin already in circulation. It is naturally countersunk, frequently respecting the original design, usually on the obverse.

Die: mirror-image matrix, incuse, impressed by a hammer blow into a metal **flan**; variously described as **cracked, corroded, repaired, worn** or **fouled**, according to its condition as detected on the coin it has produced.

Drachma: Greek precursor of the *denarius* and still the basic modern Greek denomination. It is believed originally to have denoted a 'fistful' of the iron rods (Greek: *obol/obeliskos*, a spit) used as money in Argos until the seventh century BC. An echo of the word appears in the *dram* measure. Its multiples in the Greek-speaking Roman Empire included the **(tetra)drachmon** (4) rendered in Latin as **tetradrachmum** and occasionally **tetrachmum**, the **(di)drachmon** (2) rendered in Latin as **didrachma(ta)** and a submutliple, the **(hemi)drachma** ($\frac{1}{2}$).

Exergue: segment beneath the reverse design, frequently divided from the rest of the design by a horizontal line; it often carries a **mintmark**, sometimes a brief **legend**.

Field: the plain area within the design on a coin.

Flan (French: pie or flat cake): just as in baking, the blank unstruck coin piece; variously described as **undersize, oversize, irregular, cracked, pancaked** or **bevelled**. Also known as a **blank** or **planchet**.

Flatstruck: traditional misnomer for 'unevenly struck', where the **die** has struck the **flan** at a distinct angle, leaving part of the metal only lightly impressed or even unimpressed at all. Uneven thickness around the circumference of the coin is a result of **flatstriking.**

Fourré (French: plated).

Hubmark: indentation found in the centre of both sides of many eastern bronzes: it may result from being centred in a lathe for the smoothing down of the coin edge; it may even have been a protuberance from the **die** itself, allowing for more accurate centring and steadying for the hammer blow.

Laurel: the most common type of crown on Imperial coin busts; other head adornments include the **rostral** or naval crown (Latin: **rostra**, the rambeaks of galleys), the jewelled **diadem**, the **helmet**, the **radiate** crown (Latin: *radius*, a ray) and the shroud **veil**.

Legend (Latin: *legenda*, (words) to be read): the wording on a coin.

Mint (see also **Money**): the factory producing coin, derived from the title of Juno, *Moneta*; variously described as **static** or **permanent, temporary** (to meet an emergency), **local** (as in city and provincial coinage), and **moving** (as with an army commander's HQ.)

Mintmark: sign or letters showing authority for striking or place of origin and sometimes the actual workshop and the batch from a larger mint of the later Empire. It is a form of quality control mechanism. **Open** (as opposed to **privy** or **secret**) marks again became standard by decree after the monetary reforms of *c*. AD 294. Although they had been employed during the Republic, in the intervening years of the Empire, the Imperial bust and legend had been authority mark enough for the public – at least until inflation and the growing number of usurpations of the purple undermined general confidence in the coin. Often abbreviated to *mm*, not to be confused with the measurement in millimetres.

Misstrike: General term covering **offcentre strikes** (where much of the design is missing), **mule strikes** (double headers and mismatches),

double strikes (where the design appears to be out of focus, blurred by impressions from more than one hammer blow), but most specifically used to describe a coin where the design is impressed by a second blow at an angle to the same design already struck onto the flan by a previous blow. Not to be confused with **overstrikes** where a design is struck on top of a different existing design.

Money: the word is derived from the ancient title of the goddess Juno, *Moneta*, thought to mean 'Counsellor'or even 'Alarm-raiser', a reference to the geese of the Capitol which once saved Rome and which were sacred to Juno. Juno had several titles and several temples with them, e.g. the temple of Juno Martialis on the low-lying Campus Martius near the Tiber (see Fig. 72c). That of Juno *Moneta* stood on the Capitol and since it housed the Roman mint for many years, the word *moneta* widened to embrace *coin-in-general*, coin *dies* and the *mint* itself. A *monetarius* was a coin maker or mint worker; a *monetalis* was a financial official, usually of quaestor rank in earlier times.

Numismatist (Greek: *nomisma*; Latin: *numisma*, coinage in general): A specialist in or collector of coins. *Nummus* was the Latin word for an individual coin piece, hence the words *denarius, quinarius* and *sestertius* among many others are really adjectives linked to *nummus* which was left unspoken and understood; similarly with the word *piece* in the naming of modern denominations.

Obverse and reverse: front and back, 'head and tail' of a coin; often written in old manuscript shorthand, Obv and R̭

Patina: the surface layer of oxidised metal characteristic of many ancient coins and in many cases enhancing their looks as well as acting as a protective against further reaction to the atmosphere.

Pecunia (Latin: *pecus*, cattle, farm beasts): Roman word for currency or small change, hence the word *pecuniary*. Early Rome's ingots of exchange were stamped with a design indicating the farm animal value of the metal – sheep, ox or pig.

Plating: a silver coat applied by fusion to a base core coin; less frequently it is used to describe orichalcum or other plating of a base core. Bankers' testmarks are frequently found on Roman silver and the magnifying glass almost invariably shows less formal testmarks made by the ordinary citizen. Earlier plated silver is thought by many to be official such while the border between later (second century AD) official and unofficial plating is still a matter of debate. Some scholars are increasingly inclined to the belief that all plating is unofficial and fraudulent, from whatever period of Roman coinage.

Potin (Old French: pot bronze): an alloy, usually of lead, zinc and tin with a small amount of silver ranging from 1 per cent to a maximum of 20 per cent.

Pound (Latin: *pondus*, lump or weight; *pondo*, set measure of what we now call a *pound*): the Roman pound in fact changed through the ages from ten, to twelve to sixteen *asses*; it was expressed as *libra pondo*, hence the many derivations from both these words related to the *pound*.

Radiate: name commonly used of any Roman Imperial coin which carries an obverse bust crowned with the sun's rays, the attribute of Apollo the sun god rather than an item of Imperial regalia. The long-cherished belief that the ray-crown automatically indicated a double-value coin has not gone unquestioned by some scholars. After the beginning of the fourth century the ray-crown was not used in coinage; it is, however, echoed in the traditional saint's halo of religious art.

Reduced: description of the diminished size of a coin originally introduced with a greater weight; usually used in connection with later Republican *asses* and the later *folles* of the first decades of the fourth century.

Roman: a general term covering several distinct periods of the history of Rome's influence: **Republican**, from the earliest times after the expulsion of "the kings" to *c*. 48 BC and Caesar's entry into Rome; **Republican-Imperatorial**, from Caesar's dictatorship in Rome to the decisive battle of Actium, 31 BC – during these years Rome was under *junta* rule by military leaders or *imperatores*; **Imperial**, from the battle of Actium which decided the supremacy of the *imperator* Octavian who then changed his name to the name-title *Augustus* and is regarded as the first Emperor; to the last western Emperor Romulus Augustus in AD 476; **Byzantine**, from the founding of Constantinople, AD 325 in place of the former city name, Byzantium, to AD 1453 when the eastern capital finally fell to Moslem armies.

Tooling: the re-engraving of a coin, either to enhance worn detail or to introduce new and spurious detail; also known by the French term, *ciselure*, chiselling.

Treasure trove: an English legal definition, reached by the verdict of a coroner's court, declaring that a 'treasure found' was once deliberately concealed and is therefore the property of the Crown. 'Treasure' in this ancient law in fact covers only silver or gold, but not gemstones or other metals; when found, silver or gold must be declared to a coroner for a judgment by his court; if a 'treasure trove' verdict is reached, the Crown will offer the object to a museum and the market value will go as compensation to the finder (sometimes this may be contested by the landowner). Should be object(s) not be required by a museum, the finder will regain the find for himself. Any such material is automatically forfeit to the Crown if the finder fails to report its discovery. Should the coroner's inquest decide that the 'treasure' was lost, abandoned or buried in a grave, it will not be declared 'treasure trove' and will revert to the finder. Problems arise with the advance of modern metallurgy. What exactly is silver and gold? Even lead contains minute particles of silver as does a photographic film. In 1981, an Appeal Court decision stated in a case concerning 7,000 later-third-century *antoniniani* with a 2–5 per cent silver content, that they could not be adjudged 'treasure trove' since silver content must be at least 'substantial'.

VII. Cleaning bronze and copper by electrolysis

A portion of the Bath Hoard (see Figs 40 and 65) was cleaned by this method which can remove dirt, encrustation and verdigris from base metal coins without damage to either the metal or the protective patina. Acknowledgements are due to Paul Cartwright of Bicester who has drawn collectors' attention to this formula.

Caution: some coins are beyond any cleaning; others should not be touched. It is strongly advised that the beginner experiment on low-value pieces until familiar with both the timing and the appropriate solution.

Fill a half-pint vessel (plastic, glass or pottery) with warm distilled water, then add two or three teaspoons (5 ml) of sodium sesquicarbonate (water softener) and stir. Up to 25 per cent of the solution can be made up of s.s. An electrolysis unit or similar means of converting 240 V (AC) to 12 V (DC) should then be attached to a piece of stainless steel (positive lead) and to the coin (negative lead). Immerse steel and coin in the solution, ensuring that they do not touch. After switching on the current, cleaning time varies from minutes to hours, depending on the item and the strength of solution. The coin should be checked frequently.

When the coin is free of foreign matter it should be washed using a soft brush and soap in warm, clean water and then allowed to dry over twenty-four hours in a warm place. Should white marks remain (from the sodium sesquicarbonate), these can be removed by repeating the washing stage. The coin should then be coated with beeswax and buffed with a soft brush only. The result should be aesthetically pleasing, a 'museum sheen' on the unaffected colour and patina of the coin (see Fig. 66).

While toned silver should not be cleaned, dirty and encrusted silver in some cases will respond to a mild citric acid solution (5%) instead of the sodium sesquicarbonate.

VIII. Suggestions for teachers

One of Rome's first and most notorious emperors took the throne while still of schoolboy age. In sharp contrast to this more than three hundred years later one of Rome's last emperors was a schoolmaster. The first, Nero, became at one stage the most powerful man in the known world. The second, Eugenius, is hardly remembered and was executed as an ineffectual nuisance. Fortunately schools have changed considerably – on both sides of the desk.

This book makes much of coins being tangible items and the teacher will spot an immediate tactile aid for fingertip learning. The cost, however, seems prohibitive and the chances (let alone the dangers) of taking into class a full set of Biblical coins or a fine rare specimen of a Roman *sestertius* are few. There are, of course, finely produced replicas available in museums. They are still replicas, usually one-sided, not even metal and somehow simply new and odourless. For a few pence an approximation of the real thing can be bought and can make a spellbinding contribution to a lesson. For classes on Roman Britain a worn *sestertius*, *dupondius* or *as* of Hadrian with the portrait still sufficiently distinct can easily be found on a rummage tray. A London mintmark on a Constantinian bronze could also be picked up quite cheaply, especially if the rest of the coin is poor. Fractions, *minimi* of one sort or another and the smallest but still official pre-evacuation bronzes are the most easily found. They give a good idea of the poverty of the island province in its last years.

A teacher trying to convey something of the New Testament and the time of Christ might, after reading Ch. VII, get hold of at least a worn *denarius* – they are fairly plentiful in such condition. A Roman governor's 'grape-pip' from Palestine might be too exotic to hunt down. Perhaps a *quadrans* would suffice as the next best thing. A copper *as* from any reign in the first two centuries AD will illustrate the cost of a diet of sparrows. A lesson on the Turin Shroud might be made further interesting with a worn Byzantine *follis* showing the facing figure of Christ, especially when linked with a poster of the face of the Shroud.

Obviously pupils should handle the material. If the coins are unusually good, PVC will protect them from the perspiration acid on dozens of eager but grubby figertips. Rubbings taken in exercise books and poster-size drawings on walls give pupils time to digest the objects and take something from them. Evocative questions such as 'Whose hands have these gone through?' trigger the imagination. The *sound* of an ancient coin being dropped onto a hard surface is an unusual form of eavesdropping across the centuries. The widow's farthings were dropped into a Temple collection coffer made of stone. The names of coins and the way in which some of them have survived into our own speech can also serve to sharpen pupils' awareness of language.

They will have their questions – usually about value, origin and whether they should be in a museum case. It might be worth asking the seller of the coins about their provenance. As for the museum case, there are more ancient coins than the world's museums could ever hold and this book is about enjoying the glut. The pupils will enjoy it too and money is one thing to which they will always pay attention, however long it may have been demonetised.

After a single class one day with a non-academic group of 13-year olds the following day's response was heartwarming. Like the wise men from the East they brought in their treasures – two battered replicas, a Roman lamp, two coins and a flint axehead from the garden and even two copper *asses* brought back from Africa by a parent.

In fact, there are few areas in teaching where coins cannot be used as teaching aids. They have the advantage of being cheap, simple and familiar. It is beyond the scope of this book to go into detail. Half an hour spent browsing in a dealer's shop or at a coin fair will alert the good teacher to the possibilities. The most obvious areas are geography in general, inflation, the Tudors, the French and Russian revolutions, modern Germany and the whole phenomenon known as the Crusades. Take the Armada as a final illustration. Most people know that it was the invasion fleet of Philip of Spain. How many realise that his bust appeared on England's own coin between 1554 and 1558 as the husband of Mary Tudor? By a quirk of history, some of the English sailors fighting the Armada in 1588 would have been carrying in their purses partly worn silver change bearing the head of the very man they were fighting.

INDEX

The numerals given in **bold** type refer to figure numbers. The names of emperors and certain Latin words which have not been employed in the body of the book and cannot be found in the Index may be found in the lists and glossaries under Collectors Working Information, pp. 159–81.